# T H E
# BLUE BOOK
## O F  L I F E

## The Template Guide
## After the Ring and the Parchment

*"View of Honor" Oil on Canvas by Author.*

# W. Thomas McQueeney
*The Citadel Class of 1974*

Charleston, SC
www.PalmettoPublishing.com

*The Blue Book of Life*
Copyright © 2021 by W. Thomas McQueeney

All rights reserved

Hardcover ISBN: 978-1-68515-105-8
Paperback ISBN: 978-1-63837-434-3
eBook ISBN: 978-1-63837-435-0

"When you were born, you cried and the world rejoiced. Live your life so that when you die, the world cries and you rejoice."

Cherokee Proverb

# Table of Contents

## The Blue Book of Life
### The Template Guide After the Ring and the Parchment

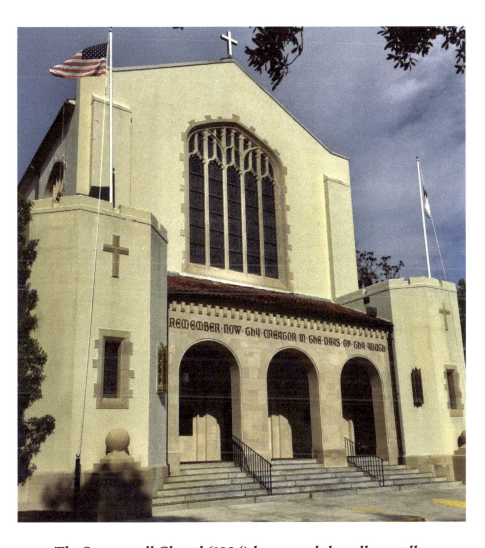

*The Summerall Chapel (1934) has served the college well—*
*especially during exams.*
*Photo by author.*

# Dedication And Acknowledgements

I dedicate this book to those who ventured forward from The Citadel, the Military College of South Carolina. They, the alumni, have forged a legacy. This dedication is as much to an institution with all of the facets of character-building concepts that have guided the lives of thousands across nearly two centuries. The Citadel experience is like a guarded secret that needs to be told.

All proceeds from this production become the property of The Citadel Foundation to benefit the extensive renovations needed for the spiritual center of the campus, Summerall Chapel. This multi-denominational chapel was built in 1936. The ceiling expanse still holds an abundance of my prayers lifted up and gathered at its apex like the escape of helium balloons at a toddler's birthday party. Many were answered. Many more were "tabled"…or in my case, "gabled." Each prayer takes time and patience to season.

The administration of The Citadel's success falls mostly under the auspices of the president, the provost, and the commandant. The Citadel Board of Visitors—the trustee board—play a major role in their guidance, and thus, in the efficacious mission of the college to produce ***principled leaders in an academic environment.***

It is essential that I acknowledge those who came forward enthusiastically to assist this effort. Two Class of 1974 friends, R. Gordon Bell and Ray Mayer, have been extraordinarily forthcoming with permissions to utilize material from "our day" in the Old Corps. Bell was the author of the famed *Fhourmations* under the pseudonym Steven T. Fhour. It is a raucous recollection of innuendo and satire from his cadet years, 1970 to 1974. Bell's sardonic humor transcends many generations of "ring knockers." Ray Mayer, an Oscar Company classmate, became a successful lawyer and prosecutor before his retirement to the hinterlands of North Georgia. His genius abilities as a Citadel cartoonist have never been matched.

Thanks go to guidance supplied by my former fellow member of The Citadel Board of Visitors, Allison Dean Love. She's still there. I'm not. I also cite the key leadership from The Citadel Foundation, Executive Director Jay Dowd, and their amazing support team. Having served eight years with that august group of selfless entrepreneurs, the TCF Board, was an honor that I will forever cherish.

Jarret Sonta deserves a stack of merit slips as he has also served in the capacity of editor—or the Herculean task of keeping me within the guidelines of the *Modern Language Association* handbook of literary style. With both an undergraduate diploma and a master's degree from Yale University, Jarret has served as Director of Communications for The Citadel Foundation for eighteen years. His abilities and his friendship are treasured.

I have benefited from my interview time with Colonel Tom Clark, USMC, Ret., '85, who serves as Executive Director of the Krause Center for Leadership and Ethics. I have also received input from a number of cadets enrolled in the 2020-2021 school year. These cadets dealt with more unknowns than knowns during the difficult time of COVID-19. They will make us all proud. It has also been my pleasure to acquaint myself with the Assistant Provost for Leadership, Dr. Faith Rivers James.

The campus perimeters and parameters have not changed much, but the protocols associated with the COVID-19 pandemic had a definitive impact upon campus life well into 2021. These were odd times to find an even keel! Indeed, the COVID-19 era will define several graduating Citadel classes. The worldwide pandemic forced the administration to stage a virtual graduation in May of 2020 and a "split-audience graduation" in May of 2021. The pandemic circumstances had all of civilization scrambling to find alternatives to normal human interaction. Despite these adverse conditions, the college found a way. It always does.

With a team of professionals committed to publishing this project, we found a way, as well. Thanks go to Jack Joseph and Erin Miller of Palmetto Publishing Group. They always seem to clear a place for me on their schedule and add valuable suggestions along the way.

*By March of 2020, protocols were enacted, and cadet life was altered for five cadet classes—from 2020 to 2024. Rendering by Ray Mayer, '74.*

I would be remiss if I did not express my appreciation for so many others within The Citadel family who have not only mentored and influenced me but assisted my post-graduate life by their continued influence.

Trying to close a dissimilarity gap of nearly fifty years would not be possible without a better understanding of The Citadel of the 2020s. That gap was closed by interviews, observations, and research that supplemented and enhanced my history of personal involvement with the college.

There is no substitute for simply speaking with today's cadets. To the cadets—now, then, and whenever again—I acknowledge their exuberance for the process of joining the long gray line. With gratitude I cite Ty'Shonna "Lilly" Jones, '23, and Hayden Brown, '21, for their participation, among others. There was much insight to be gained in the interaction with the Cadet Corps.

*The Class of 2007 Summerall Guards form up for the halftime performance at the University of Pittsburgh September 23, 2006. Photo by author.*

The Citadel is wider, longer, and deeper than its graduate numbers would indicate. The influence of Corps of Cadets everywhere is astonishing. The Citadel is further heightened by the success of The Citadel Graduate College and their esteemed alumni, many of whom were once cadets…and many others who arrived from elsewhere and enjoyed the focused sense of our campus life. Proudly, The Citadel has also provided other programs – for American military veterans as undergraduates, military enlisted commissioning programs, and a community-beneficial "2 plus 2" program that assists associate degree holders from technical colleges.

Many years ago, I was traveling south on Interstate 75 between Knoxville and Chattanooga, Tennessee. A motorist pulled behind me and began flashing his lights. Concerned that I may have a low tire or some other unknown calamity imminent, I pulled over to the shoulder. The older gentleman exited his vehicle with a broad and friendly smile. He had noticed my Citadel Alumni rear window sticker and wanted to meet me. He was from a class from the early 1960s. He thought nothing about stopping on a dangerous truck-laden interstate to have the opportunity to meet another graduate. We exchanged pleasantries and moved on. Over the years, I had often thought about that incident. Do alums from Georgia Tech or Slippery Rock do that? Probably not. Baylor? Cal State Fullerton? Notre Dame? I doubt that these fine colleges have that heightened institutional attachment. The interstate incident reminded me that our bond is unique.

My last acknowledgement is to all who wear the ring. We have a lifetime to fulfill its promise.

# Foreword

This book is not limited to the experiences of cadets at The Citadel but does focus on the precepts of what is available in that elevated four-year course study of how one might gain a rewarding life. Think of this short book as a way to distill what is learned in a small Southern institution in a manner that can be interpolated to the masses. The four-year cadet experience is focused and touches on nearly every element of highly cherished goals for anyone's life. The fact that a Citadel cadet is able to concentrate on a course of study to implement a burgeoning career could be looked at as the certificate bonus of the enterprise. The Citadel experience consists of such valued instruction beyond the academic degree requirements that it has inspired this work.

The flaws and foibles of mankind often disrupt the course of a good and decent life. Our heroes are—too often—sports celebrities, entertainers, movie stars, and politicians. There are sometimes even heroes of fiction. It could be said, instead, that the true heroes of our existence are nearer to us. They are our mothers, brothers, sisters, and dads. They are soldiers, ministers, teachers, doctors, counselors, and engineers. And they likely transcend all class and economic strata because they foster the virtues of decency, truth, and service to others.

***Storm over Bond Hall 2014.***
***Photo by author.***

The *Blue Book* is used as a symbol. *The Citadel Blue Book* is a set of rules that were devised in an orderly fashion to guide a Citadel cadet through his or her four years of substantive and well-rounded learning—both inside and outside of the classroom. The *Blue Book* expanded and contracted with the times, within its scope of discipline. For instance, cadets of fifty years ago did not have cell phones or computers. Pages were added. They did have electric fans and common-use single-gender bathrooms. Pages were deleted. Regardless of the times, the *Blue Book* set out a detailed discourse to define proper behavior, with the potential result of disciplinary action should that code of discipline fail to be sustained.

Offenses were categorized. They were the sins against the system. The stoic and sterile manual anticipated nearly every aberration. It was unlikely that an 18-year-old would have been accustomed to such a restrictive venue from his or her previous upbringing. Universally, The Citadel posed a rigid new order of consequence in the stark manual published to define the college's requirements of conduct. This production is not meant to assume a biased view that cadet graduates become model citizens and exemplary human beings simply as a result of the training. That happens often but is not a given. This book instead underscores that the template for a rewarding and beneficial life beyond The Citadel has been emplaced, and that the life that the cadet-graduate leads can then become his or her legacy. It is up to each individual accordingly. The precepts of a good life lived are admirably attained from a variety of backgrounds well outside of The Citadel's realm. The journey within merely foists the consistent opportunity of virtue that the college provides.

Much of the book is devoted to bringing back the meaningful moments that comprised four years of character growth—from the trepidation of matriculation to the exuberance of graduation. Thus, the photos within become an intentional and poignant reminder of those times. They are meant to maneuver the mind to all tenets of a cadet career—academic, spiritual, physical, military, and within the barracks relationships one would garner. It is those moments that solidified the profound integrity, the myriad skills, and the confident attitude of determination to be utilized in a lifetime.

The campus humor became its own condiment sprinkled on the main course. We should never take ourselves too seriously. The Blue Book of discipline rarely inhibited the individual personalities of the cadets who arrived from fifty states and several foreign countries. That code book had more of an odd unifying impact. Cadets found ways to whistle through rainstorms and laugh away pain.

*"Martha, they say these cadets are a bit different.*
*Don't get too close."*
**From the Mind of Ray Mayer.**

There is much more influence about this journey to understand. No one does it alone.

The four years pass by quickly. Suddenly, a *22-ish,* academically accomplished cadet is awarded a diploma. He or she may be profoundly convinced that the flash of the ring will open every door. In fact, the ring will open a few tantalizing avenues for success, but not the wide boulevards. Those steps toward the light can only be initiated by the wearer. Take heed. And take notes.

This publication is not intended to be a compendium of well-researched facts, but rather an advisory source that may help one to help oneself. The symbolic avenues that lie ahead could lead equally to dusty back alleyways or to exciting streets paved with sapphires and amethyst.

It's natural to remain skeptical of a writer's lofty appraisal of your future. Parenthetically, I wish I were standing in your place today, yet knew the elements of Citadel values as well as I know them now.

I'm part of the older "Old Corps." The president of the college who presented my diploma graduated in 1932! Though that gap may indicate a wider loss of understanding and appreciation for today's Citadel graduate, be assured that I have stayed "in touch" and engaged. Fortunately, I was elected by the South Carolina state legislature to serve on our college's Board of Visitors. I also served concurrently on The Citadel Foundation Board of Directors during my six-year BOV term. And concurrent to those roles, I had been serving (more than three decades as of 2021) as the Class of 1974's TCF class chairman. Through all of this involvement, my most rewarding role has been to serve as a mentor to dozens of cadets over many years. Undertaking this enterprise is part of my soul. There may be higher callings, but few higher passions. You matter. I love The Citadel and deeply appreciate the blessings my four-year experience has entailed and delivered.

*"Chill, man. He said he had to be back by midnight.*
*I only missed by four hours."*
**From the Mind of Ray Mayer.**

Just a brief reference to my cadet career for its irony: I was not a sterling cadet. At least I never considered myself as such. I did not attend The Citadel on an academic scholarship or military contract. Scholarships were scarce in my day. The Vietnam War was winding down. I was an Air Force ROTC student with awful eyesight—not likely a pilot candidate. I did manage to hold rank over my last three years—but I viewed that fact with deference. I never gave out a demerit. So many cadets in my company were not academically eligible for rank—so the Jenkins Hall ROTC tactical leadership was stuck with me. I never "got busted" and never walked a tour. I'm not suggesting that I never applied my own rationalization to the rules and skirted many along the way. I just never got caught. Admittedly, I left the campus several times in the trunk of a car. That Blue Book infraction is among the most egregious and harshly punished—A.W.O.L., **A**way **W**ith**o**ut **L**eave. I'm still smirking today as the tours and confinements are not retroactive.

*The author…when the standards were much lower.*

I was an English major and *barely* an honor graduate. My shoes and my brass were in the *OMG* state of neglect. My focus as a cadet was on intramural sports and my academic major. I tried to walk on to The Citadel basketball team but was "cut" because I had the worst jump shot imaginable. They went on to an 11-15 record without the benefit of having me languish on the far end of the bench. I served as the Sports Editor of *The Brigadier* and won several writing awards from our local newspaper and from other collegiate journalism sources. But my passion for the written word was waylaid by other responsibilities—the repayment of multiple student loans. I graduated on a mid-May Saturday and flew to Atlanta that Sunday to start my career in finance on Monday. I didn't return to journalism until 2011. If you're counting, that's a 37-year hiatus. Since 2011, I have written and published fourteen books. Well, this is the fifteenth.

'Nuff said. Let's talk about you.

You have a unique toolbox. In fact, of all colleges across the land, your toolbox is bigger, more diverse, and more adaptive than any other. We're going to explore that toolbox for what it contains with respect to every life situation to come.

There may be exceptions among us, but The Citadel graduate typically completes the arduous and challenging multifaceted curriculum in four years. Who wants to stick around any longer? Did you know that The Citadel either leads the nation or is near the top of the national statistics annually for four-year graduation rates? It's a cultural thing. Cadets want to get their rings and graduate with their class. Exceptions occur and are acknowledged here. Getting that diploma in four years or a bit beyond does not diminish the effort and perseverance it takes to do so. And there are those who can shorten even that rigorous demand. My oldest son, Billy McQueeney, '99, graduated from The Citadel in three years as a Gold Star (accumulative 3.7 GPA plus) student! A better man than me, he played on the basketball team!

*Effort* and *perseverance* are in your toolbox.

Just making the college-choice decision to be challenged cannot go unacknowledged. In doing so, statistically, a modern cadet recruit is chosen among the top 20% of high school students who apply. Yes, The Citadel is in great demand. Stated in reverse, The Citadel Admissions Office turns away more than 80% of those who apply with each incoming class. They chose you, and you made that choice a wise one.

We can already add *high and daunting purpose* to your toolbox. If you were like me before matriculating, you probably had no idea what you were about to experience. But you did know that you were entering a highly regimented system that allowed very little outside engagement with the "real world" beyond Lesesne Gate. You may have known that you would wear a uniform and be required to meet standards of physical fitness. You did know that the academic demands would be daunting and would require additional ROTC credits, whether you planned a military career or not. You did know that you would have other military requirements, such as drill and dress parades and room inspections. You knew that your study time, ESP (Evening Study Period), would be ingrained into your daily schedule. You knew that you would be taking orders from young people who were contemporaneous—and who could be overbearing at times. You made a decision to subject yourself to an arduous and unrelenting fourth-class system.

How did you get through it? I'll give you the word used for that critical tool, as well. *Determination.* How do I know? There's an analogy I used back in 2012, when I was asked to address the Daniel Scholars Luncheon in Buyer Auditorium at Mark Clark Hall. It's in a later chapter. When you get there, you'll see it is an undeniable point that a Citadel graduate has a deep sense of determination.

Your weighty toolbox has others. You can ***overcome adversity***. You arrived in August and reached Recognition Day successfully in the toughest plebe system in America. The grueling experience was hourly, daily, and weekly. Knob year is the pits! But you exhibited the mettle to succeed.

General Mark Wayne Clark served as president of The Citadel from 1954 to 1965. General Clark once stated, "Whatever we do in life, we must look back and be proud." That brand of pride cannot be admonished, but rather saluted. One must not fall into the chasm of haughtiness, pomposity, smugness, and conceit. Our collective and individual flaw is our imperfection and our history of errors against our own good judgement. We are distinctively human. We'll have regrets because we'll all have failures. Sometimes I feel like I'm leading the league in several dismal categories. But I'm encouraged that there is a better day and a better way ahead.

*Bond Hall is the administrative center point of The Citadel.*

There are other tools we will delineate for clarity—*ethics* and ***honor***, ***time management***, an ***adherence to duty***, an understanding of ***leadership*** and chain-of-command, ***respect for others***, ***discipline***, and ***ingenuity***. And these are not all!

These are the tools most sought by employers. They are also the tools most sought by a prospective spouse, friends, and business associates. Mind you, these are also the characteristics that often build entrepreneurship, problem solving, and perspective. Would you trust a mechanic who showed up for work with just a screwdriver and a wrench? Or would you prefer the mechanic who rolled out a four-hundred-pound professional toolbox with a dozen deep drawers? Add in that the prepared mechanic is likely one who arrived on time and in the proper attire…

The following chapters will help you find other assets that will enable you to raise *our* Citadel-enhanced collective impact upon our communities—and our country, as well. Yes, you represent all of us. The mindset is to advance and achieve.

Throughout the text it will be necessary to intersperse the third-person narrative form with the first-person form of individual insight. My sense is that there are incidents, events, and activities with which we can all identify—regardless of the number specified on that cherished golden ring.

When you walked across that stage and the president of the college handed you the parchment, you completed your toolbox set.

Now, let's build something.

*Next challenge? I got this!*
*From the Mind of Ray Mayer.*

# Section One: The Cadet Experience

May we agree that the trajectory plotted early will allow the greatest chance of completing the mission and arriving at the destination desired? There are basic fundamentals to be achieved in what has been a positive crucible for life's journey—The Citadel experience. Many of these fundamentals may have been well-ingrained from the household of a young adult taking the next step in his or her development. But regardless of the circumstances of one's early years, The Citadel allows a format to build upon a value system to be used for a lifetime.

The cadet experience is analogous to a journey plotted. Achievement is built upon who we were, who we are, and who we can become. There is no static condition—only growth and progress.

To begin the journey, we must come to know the key details about the starting point and its purpose. For that reason, a short history is appropriate.

*"Really?  Who looks there?"*
*From the Mind of Ray Mayer.*

# The Perspective of Citadel History

So, why did The Citadel come into being?

There's recorded history, there's revisionist history, and then there's eyewitness history. And sometimes there's an amalgam of the three. Yet, we often lean toward the version that best suits our purpose. It's best to walk through what we know to be true, with care to notate what may likely be conjecture.

Fact: The Citadel Academy was established in 1842 by the South Carolina Legislature. But academic instruction did not begin until the first cadets reported on March 20, 1843. There was a "brother" institution—The Arsenal Academy— in Columbia, SC. By 1845, The Arsenal Academy began training first-year cadets before sending them to Charleston for their final three years. The Arsenal was burned down at the command of Union General William Tecumseh Sherman in February of 1865 and never re-emerged. The only building spared from the original Arsenal in that Civil War calamity now serves as the South Carolina Governor's Mansion.[1]

Another fact: The Citadel and The Arsenal in Columbia occupied then-existing buildings that housed munitions for military use. Both facilities were improved. The Charleston facility had previously been a tobacco warehouse. Both were manned by young soldiers serving a defensive military mission related to the Denmark Vesey slave uprising in Charleston (1822). The institution of African to West-Indian to Charleston slave trade festered until its abolishment after the horrible epoch of its impact upon the history of the Western Hemisphere. The Denmark Vesey uprising postured an organized protective response over the next twenty years. The "Old Citadel" structure in its former purpose was simply a barracks to house young men charged with that protective responsibility.

Once the State Legislature commissioned these two state arsenal locations for higher education, the barracks were upgraded (again), and classrooms added. For the next seventeen years, both munition arsenals became colleges. And in his message delivered to the State Legislature on December 20, 1842, articulating the purpose of the two academies, the governor, John P. Richardson, saw the potential:

> *If the success of these institutions should form the basis of future and important improvements, which may judiciously be extended to our free schools; if they should supply better teachers from their alumni; if they should suggest higher standards and better systems of morals;…or if they only awaken greater ardor in the people, and a warmer interest in our rulers, to advance the cause of education; they will achieve more for the weal and honor of our State than all the other labors and appliances of government could in any other manner confer.[2]*

And then the cadets started a war. Yes, that was our cadets. Food fights weren't enough. So, it was a cadet detachment from The Citadel charged with manning an artillery battery on Morris Island who fired upon the Star of the

West—a Union resupply ship. The Star of the West was a food and munitions ship sent to assist the federal garrison at Fort Sumter. Shots were fired in warning. The ship turned around and sailed away. In effect, those volleys lit the kindling of the colossal conflagration. It turned out to be the most miserable episode in our country's history. Ostensibly, our cadets who fired those shots were simply doing as directed by their superiors.

Just three months later, on April 12, 1861, Confederate General P.G.T. Beauregard made the war official. A 34-hour bombardment of Fort Sumter produced a peaceful surrender. No lives were lost in the battle, and no prisoners were taken. In fact, the Union troops were saluted and allowed to return north. But 620,000 lives were lost in the ensuing four years.[3] Citadel cadets and graduates were involved in numerous battles of that war, and many are counted among the nation's tally of lives lost.

After the Civil War, The Citadel facility was still (generally) intact on Marion Square. Occupied by Union Forces in 1865, the campus housed federal troops during Reconstruction. The Arsenal Academy in Columbia was abandoned. By 1879, The Citadel "Academy" on Marion Square was turned back into its 1842 purpose as a military college and reopened in 1882. Some four decades later, in 1922, the college moved to its new campus on the banks of the Ashley River, where it remains today.

In time prosperity returned, and Citadel graduates became renowned for their discipline, reliability, and well-rounded academic ability. The college produced leaders in every field.

Why was The Citadel allowed to continue its mission after the Civil War? How does it survive and thrive? Why are admissions to this small military college "maxed out" each and every year?

History is an inarguable indicator. The need that The Citadel fulfilled exceeded the reasons for its dissolution.

Several U.S. presidents (and future presidents) visited The Citadel over its luminous history. Those included Franklin Delano Roosevelt, who was not initially aware that The Citadel had moved its campus thirteen years before he spoke:

> *When I heard that I was to speak at The Citadel, old memories came back to me, memories not only of my own visit to the old school, but also of the great historic tradition of that school—an historical record, a war record, if you please, of The Citadel boys that ought to be known to every boy in the United States. Then when I learned that The Citadel had moved, somehow I got a little choky over it, wondering what it would be like; and yet here I come and I find the old Citadel reproduced. It is reproduced, I am confident, for generations to come, for the continuance of this splendid institution. I am happy indeed that you have moved it here to these very fitting surroundings, and that The Citadel is under the command of my old friend General Summerall. . . .[4]*

Other presidents who came to visit and speak to the elite and distinguished Corps of Cadets include Theodore

Roosevelt, Herbert Hoover, Dwight D. Eisenhower, Gerald Ford, Ronald Reagan, George W. Bush, Barack Obama, and Donald Trump. Indeed, the Corps of Cadets has become an audience for those in power or seeking political capital for a future presidential bid.

The Citadel story is one of Spartan beginnings. The Military College of South Carolina has become a bastion of self-discipline, learning, and achievement. The story bears these facts:

- Militarily, The Citadel supplied officers and soldiers to every major conflict from the Mexican-American War to the nation's current conflicts. The Citadel lost 49 graduates and 200 cadets fighting on both sides of the Civil War.[5] A Citadel War Memorial has been erected between the Daniel Library and Mark Clark Hall to commemorate The Citadel's sacrifices of military personnel throughout its history.

- On three occasions, entire cadet classes joined a war effort. The first was the Civil War. The other two: the Class of 1918 (World War I) and the Class of 1944 (World War II), the latter of which came to be known as "the Class that Never Was." More than 6,000 Citadel alumni saw combat in World War II, 209 of whom paid the ultimate sacrifice either directly in combat or from wounds received.[6]

- The Citadel annually supplies more U. S. Army officers to our nation's military than any other national educational institution outside of the United States Military Academy at West Point.

And then other traditions and advancements inured the strategically located Military College of South Carolina that elevated the prowess of its national reach. The process to become today's Citadel had growing pains.

- The Cadet Honor Code was established in 1919. While its enforcement ebbed and flowed until formally reestablished by General Mark Clark in 1955, the essence of the code has not changed in a century: "A cadet does not lie, cheat, or steal, nor tolerate those who do." The code's restrictions exceed those of the U.S. military academies and is enforced by senior cadets elected by their peers to serve on the Honor Committee to adjudicate alleged violations.

- Currently, nearly one-third of all Citadel graduates enter the five military services each year (to include the United States Army, Navy, Air Force, Marines, and Coast Guard).

- The first African American cadet, Charles Foster, entered The Citadel in 1966. Yet The Citadel had registered its first Chinese students in the 1920s and Thai students in the 1950s. By 2020, the minority cadet population reached 23%.[7]

- The first two female graduates, Nancy Mace and Petra Lovetinska (Class of 2000) were roommates who matriculated together. Mace, who graduated in three years, went on to become the Congressional 1st District Representative from South Carolina, and Lovetinska (m. Seipel) served the Marine Corps as a career officer.

*Bronze Bust of Alvah H. Chapman, Jr.*

*The Class of 1942 Regimental Commander received the Distinguished Flying Cross as a hero of World War II. He found professional success as the Chairman and CEO of Knight-Ridder Newspapers in Miami, Florida, where a major boulevard is named in his honor.*

- Other notable Citadel alumni include 38-year U.S. Senator Fritz Hollings; author Pat Conroy; Thomas Dry Howie (The Major of St. Lo); author Robert Jordan

(James O. Rigney); Governor John C. West; entrepreneur Harvey Schiller; NFL football player and TV sports analyst Paul Maguire; technology executive and venture capitalist Bill Krause; opera performer Morris Robinson; Charleston's 40-year mayor Joseph P. Riley, Jr.; Country Music Hall-of-Famer Tandy Rice; country singer Mitchell Lee; businessman Bill Sansom; attorney Gene Moore; dozens of professional sports athletes (including the NFL's Stump Mitchell and Andre Roberts, along with MLB pitchers Britt Reames and Asher Wojciechowski), newspaper syndicate chairman Alvah Chapman, and numerous military leaders, several of who returned to serve as presidents of the college—Oliver Bond, 1886; James Duckett, '32; George Seignious, '42; James A. Grimsley, '42; Claudius "Bud" Watts III, '58; John Rosa, '73; and Glenn Walters, '79.

- Two long-serving non-graduate presidents of The Citadel—General Charles P. Summerall and General Mark W. Clark—assumed major historical roles in wartime (Summerall in WWI, Clark in WWII). General Clark is buried on The Citadel campus.

- The official name was changed in 1919 to "The Citadel, the Military College of South Carolina." The word "Academy" was dropped.[8]

- The Citadel Class of 2012 featured female first- and second-honor graduates (equivalent to valedictorian and salutatorian), though the female cadet population is consistently below ten percent of the Corps of Cadets. The first female Regimental Commander was Sarah J. Zorn, '19.

- The Citadel Beach House (by way of an Aiken, SC estate gift) was funded by *The Chicago Tribune* publisher COL Robert R. McCormick, USA, who did not attend The Citadel but served under GEN Charles P. Summerall in World War I.[9]

*Classmates from 1989: Basketball coach Ed Conroy and astronaut Randy Bresnik.*
*Photo by author.*

- "The man who handed the rope" after the Air Florida Flight 90 crash into the Potomac River in 1982 was Citadel graduate Arland D. Williams, Jr., '57. When a rescue helicopter arrived, Williams heroically passed the lifeline to save the lives of five fellow passengers before perishing himself with the submersion of the plane. The 14th Street Bridge in Washington is named in his honor.[10]

- Lt Col Charles D. Hodges, '00, accepted a royal decoration from the Kingdom of Thailand in ceremonies at the Royal Thai Embassy in Washington, D.C. Hodges received the honor for his participation as the U. S. Air Force on-scene commander at the Tham Luang cave rescue in northern Thailand in 2018, during which a team of young Thai soccer players and their coach were recovered safely. Hodges's family, including his father, Rev. Richard Hodges, USAF, Ret., '72, and his brother, Joe Hodges, '07, attended the ceremony with him.[11]

- A series of paintings extolling pre-1922 cadet life on the campus at Marion Square were commissioned and are displayed at the President's Office in Bond Hall. These oil paintings were completed by famed Charleston artist Alicia Rhett (1915-2014), who also famously starred as India Wilkes in the 1939 blockbuster film *Gone with the Wind*. A talented stage actress, she withdrew from acting to devote her life to her art.

- The Citadel athletic teams have a proud history. The Citadel baseball team shocked the sports world by making it to the NCAA College World Series in 1991 as the smallest enrollment participant in modern NCAA history...still. The football Bulldogs have achieved the #1 ranking in FCS football (1992) and have beaten or tied six much larger programs in away contests in their respective state capital cities—Vanderbilt, Richmond, Florida State, Georgia Tech, Navy, and South Carolina.

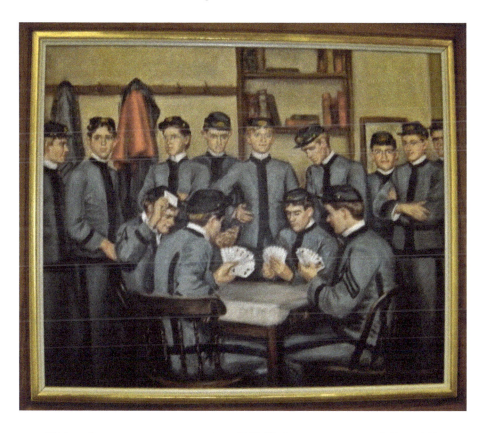

*This oil painting gracing Bond Hall depicts campus life at The Citadel on Marion Square prior to the college's move to the Ashley River in 1922. The artist was Charlestonian Alicia Rhett who also starred in the classic film* **Gone with the Wind.**

## *...And a Few Other Foundation Points*

The history is compelling. To understand the mystique about The Citadel and its extraordinary impact upon the nation, it is essential to recognize the mindset of its graduates.

The Citadel boasts a strong sense of giving back from alumni. Among the early prominent gifts was the Daniel Fund family of scholarships. These needs-based packages originated from two brothers' large construction firm in Greenville, SC. Chares E. (Class of 1918) and R. Hugh Daniel (Class of 1929) wanted to do something significant. They did! The Daniel Fund Scholarship has assisted hundreds of cadets over several generations. The Daniel brothers started a tradition of giving back that resonates profoundly in today's Citadel family.

The Citadel story is expanding continuously as key graduates such as Tommy Baker, '72, Gene Moore, '58, and Bill Sansom, '64, dedicated substantial sums to support educational and athletic programs. Bill Krause, '63, along with his wife Gay Krause, founded the Krause Leadership Initiative in the early 2000s that has since become a center housing the college's leadership development programs. Every cadet has access to this experience-enhancer. Bill Endictor, '58, bequeathed an impressive estate gift to better the college for the coming century. The Swain brothers, Dave '80, and Chris '81, have named and endowed notable campus facilities and academic programs through cash and estate gifts. Charleston business owner and philanthropist Anita Zucker donated the lead gift to name and endow the Zucker Family School of

Education. Other major donors have given of their time and talent in addition to providing significant funds. The historic attitude of selfless generosity by key Citadel-centric philanthropists has vaulted the college to national prominence.

*The Citadel first new building since 1974 opened in 2021. Bastin Hall houses The Tommy & Victoria Baker School of Business. Photo by author.*

Bastin Hall has been funded by private philanthropy thanks to a lead gift of more than $6 million by the largesse of Mary Lee and Rick Bastin, '65. This new home for the Tommy and Victoria Baker School of Business is the first new academic edifice constructed on The Citadel's campus since 1974. Another project, the new Capers Hall – where one would find the Liberal Arts departments of English, modern languages, history, and psychology—should be completed by the summer of 2023.

The Citadel Foundation continues to assist the administration by its efforts to re-attach alumni and friends to the *cause célèbre* of the institution.

Founded in 1961, The Citadel Development Foundation, as it was originally known, was chartered exclusively to fund academic programs, with no purview over athletic development or bricks-and-mortar capital projects. In the interest of expanding this restrictive role and merging other campus fundraising efforts within the same organization, the bylaws and name were changed in 2000 to create The Citadel Foundation (TCF). Following this consolidation, TCF has been tasked to oversee all fundraising with the exception of Citadel Athletics scholarships and memberships. TCF has since become the college's leading benefactor, and its wide success is often credited with expanding The Citadel's educational prowess, as financial support from the State of South Carolina – once the college's primary funding source — typically amounts to less than ten percent of the college's $150 million-plus annual budget today. It has been the inestimable work of The Citadel Foundation, in concert with the college administration and through the generosity of donors, that has enhanced the college's prominence on the national stage.

The expansion of Citadel academic disciplines has roots in the changing needs of society. Recent programs have been developed in systems engineering, nursing, sports management, intelligence and security studies, and cybersecurity. As an institution dedicated to developing principled leaders, the college offers a minor in Leadership Studies among its 50-plus minor and 30-plus major courses of study.

The Citadel is steeped in history and traditions, but the college's role is ever adaptive and ever changing. Graduates become part of a reputational reach that signals perseverance, leadership, and ethics. Often found in short supply in society at large, these characteristics remain universally valued and in constant need.

*Corps of Cadet avocations are intense.*
*"Move aside, fresh can."*
*From the Mind of Ray Mayer.*

## *The Four Years You'll Never Forget*

Though common threads bind our experiences, the cadets in the current generation are quite different than those of five decades ago. First of all, they'd likely be more academically suited. A brief history of The Citadel's growth is in order.

The Corps of Cadets of the 1970s was reputed to be "two-thousand strong," but the actual number was much less. Cadet populations in the 1970s were rather static, at 1600 to 1700 cadets. Only four barracks housed the Corps, and it was rare to have over one hundred cadets in any of the seventeen companies extant.

The early 1970s were defined by converging social conditions that impacted The Citadel's lagging enrollment. Primary among those social issues was the war in Vietnam. Military colleges were not popular during the Vietnam years as the nightly news reported the hardened results, including nearly 47,000 war deaths.[12] This grim roster of fatalities included 76 Citadel alumni.[13] Since many of these casualties were concurrent to those early 1970's enrollments, the impact became decidedly serious and heartfelt, even in the Corps of Cadets. Occasionally, a cadet casualty in the Vietnam theater was announced at the evening mess, accompanied by a moment of silence. This became a solemn and horrific reminder of the world beyond the enclave of cream-colored Moorish architecture.

Other factors affected enrollment as well. The new counterculture brought in a full generation of college-age "baby

18

boomers" who found the benefits of a military college some-what less attractive. The illegal drug culture grew. The Women's Liberation movement began. The first Earth Day brought ecology to the forefront in 1970. There was the silli-ness of "free love" and "streaking." But the most society-alter-ing movement of the times was well overdue—Civil Rights. This intersection of the Vietnam War, the Civil Rights move-ment, and the myriad components of the counterculture made the highly restrictive life of a cadet synonymous with watching history being made through a window. With the exception of the natural military track to potential Vietnam service, the world passed by the Corps of Cadets in the early 1970s. The campus insulated much from the world outside of Lesesne Gate.

That's not to say that that Old Corps did not make the most of those four years. They shared many of the same experienc-es that those of recent cadet vintage have enjoyed. There were senior parties, a ring ceremony, rank boards, and Summerall Guard performances. There were Greater Issues speakers, an array of Mess Hall misbehaviors, and mock ceremonies when a senior officer was busted. The stories and cartoons (and *Dear John* Letters) were in *The Brigadier*, the art and prose in *The Shako*, and cadet career accomplishments cited in *The Sphinx*. Carefully crafted ERWs were essential components of the life and times of a cadet, as they are today. Like the current Corps, cadets of former times traded off guard duty and bummed vehicle rides to downtown establishments. We all, then and now, learned much about ourselves. We found out that our dark humor was appreciated because we were all in the same situation. We found that we had tremendous, interconnected support when we leaned on each other. That bond lasts a lifetime.

*"Abort Invasion. I repeat…abort invasion.*
*Unpredictable life forms present."*
*From the Mind of Ray Mayer.*

Make no mistake, that cadet experience of the past was not exactly the same as the one currently provided. A sure bet is that the members of the Corps from yesteryear had lower SAT scores and a more difficult path to advance academically without the modern nuances. Imagine late nights at the Daniel Library with the Dewey Decimal System in lieu of a click on Google. Indeed, that age had few academic career options available for the nearly 55% of us who were graduating as 2nd lieutenants and ensigns. That's right, 55%. Most cadets contracted to join the military.

Civil Engineering was a five-year program for most. More than half of the 1970s cadet graduates were business majors. There was a smattering of Math, English, History, Political Science, Physical Education, and Biology or Chemistry. Compare those avenues with today's Citadel academic discipline choices! Today's Corps enjoys the option to choose from a vast menu of academic opportunities.

The major commonality from then to now is and will always be the four-year experience together in the battalions. It is within this experience that one will gain key lifelong friendships. You'll remember your roommates always—especially from your knob year. You will remember the hard stuff, yes—but it will be the funny stuff that makes you smile. You'll remember getting caught for something you thought to be egregious at the moment but realized its triviality when considered over time. And you'll remember what you got away with as being monumental when—at any other regular college—it would be interpreted as routine. We share these experiences with you, as other classes that graduated many years prior shared with us. True across generations, these universal experiences are what makes a Citadel ring glisten with distinction over a lifetime.

There is much that was gained and will be gained by and by.

*Hayden Brown made himself into a top NCAA basketball player.*
*His cadet experience superseded his athletic exploits.*
*Photo courtesy Charleston Post & Courier.*

A 2021 graduate, Hayden Brown played basketball for the Bulldogs, served as team captain, and attained the accolade of becoming a first-team All-Southern-Conference performer. He led the league in scoring and rebounding and has the second most double-doubles (double-figure points and rebounds in the same game) in the college's history. But his Cadet Corps interaction with others at The Citadel stands well beyond his individual honors.

*My growth as a cadet has been exponential, not just in my manhood and maturity, but in my relationships with others. I've learned what it truly means to love others well – my friends and family. I have found so many new friends here in the classroom and in the barracks and even across sports like volleyball and track. My experience has not been what I thought I'd get out of it when I first chose The Citadel. It is much more. The structure fosters accountability in every part of life. I'm learning to break down controversy to find solutions. Most importantly, my journey through The Citadel has been rooted in finding Jesus Christ and building a relationship with Him, slowly molding me into the man He's called me to be. I can't imagine I would have been able to grow as much as an individual anywhere else. Hayden Brown, '21*

Indeed, Brown relates much of the personal attitude that comprises the full Citadel experience. That growth period from high school graduate to college graduate may be uniquely administered to each, but the comprehensive and immersive activities live well past the ring and the parchment.

The four years shared stand out. These are landmark experiences for all times. A grad will cite a moment, a conversation, an event, or even a travesty within an environment so unique that it paints the picture in vivid colors, always. And those four years produce companions who recognize the same vibrant colors. You'll know those individuals warmly as ***classmates***.

The word classmate may be your most dependable tool for a lifetime. The sense of the word *classmate* grows with time to become likened to *family* or *insider* or *confidant*. It holds more conviction than the same word used at other institutions because it has a deeper and more trusted meaning as the years fly by. A classmate is someone who will come to another classmate's aid, come what may. It is a special designation at The Citadel that shines brighter as time dims the road ahead. The number on the ring places a classmate at the ready to prove consequential to other classmates, unequivocally and devotedly. And that bond only gets better with age!

*Job interviews tilted decidedly toward the wearer of the ring.*
*From the Mind of Ray Mayer.*

# A Visual Trip Down Nostalgia Way

For many of us, The Citadel required instant focus, concentration, and adaptability. With thanks to the Daniel Library, The Post & Courier, and several electronic public sources, the cursory documents and historical photographs are shown below.

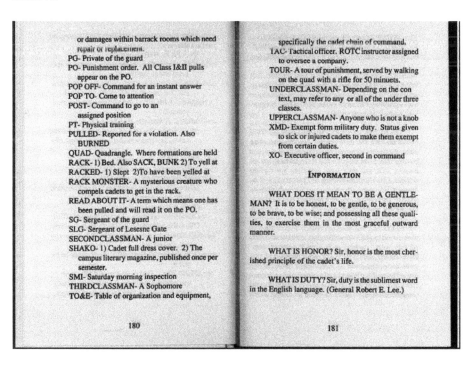

or damages within barrack rooms which need repair or replacement.

PG- Private of the guard

PO- Punishment order. All Class I&II pulls appear on the PO.

POP OFF- Command for an instant answer

POP TO- Come to attention

POST- Command to go to an assigned position

PT- Physical training

PULLED- Reported for a violation. Also BURNED

QUAD- Quadrangle. Where formations are held

RACK- 1) Bed. Also SACK, BUNK 2) To yell at

RACKED- 1) Slept 2)To have been yelled at

RACK MONSTER- A mysterious creature who compels cadets to get in the rack.

READ ABOUT IT- A term which means one has been pulled and will read it on the PO.

SG- Sergeant of the guard

SLG- Sergeant of Lesesne Gate

SECONDCLASSMAN- A junior

SHAKO- 1) Cadet full dress cover. 2) The campus literary magazine, published once per semester.

SMI- Saturday morning inspection

THIRDCLASSMAN- A Sophomore

TO&E- Table of organization and equipment,

specifically the cadet chain of command,

TAC- Tactical officer. ROTC instructor assigned to oversee a company.

TOUR- A tour of punishment, served by walking on the quad with a rifle for 50 minuets.

UNDERCLASSMAN- Depending on the con text, may refer to any or all of the under three classes.

UPPERCLASSMAN- Anyone who is not a knob

XMD- Exempt form military duty. Status given to sick or injured cadets to make them exempt from certain duties.

XO- Executive officer, second in command

### INFORMATION

WHAT DOES IT MEAN TO BE A GENTLE-MAN? It is to be honest, to be gentle, to be generous, to be brave, to be wise; and possessing all these qualities, to exercise them in the most graceful outward manner.

WHAT IS HONOR? Sir, honor is the most cherished principle of the cadet's life.

WHAT IS DUTY? Sir, duty is the sublimest word in the English language. (General Robert E. Lee.)

180                    181

The benefit of having different and highly capable presidents, provosts, and commandants register their influence, along with the rotations of personnel on the college's trustee board, The Citadel Board of Visitors, has brought he Citadel forward. The campus jargon has remained mostly constant, but the societal advancements have defined much generational change.  Much evidentiary information can be found in the old publications and the well-preserved artifacts f The Citadel Museum.

## Mess Carver Responsibility
### Chapter 4 Blue Book

- The table Mess Carver (Commander/Team Captain) for 4C cadets will be a cadet officer or a junior class sword bearing NCO who has attended and completed the Commandant's Mess Carver Certification Training.

- Mess Carvers for other than fourth class messes will be cadet officers, first class privates, or junior sword bearers, only.

- During the cadre period no other upper-class cadet will sit at a knob mess. After Parent's Weekend 4C will be integrated into their company tables.  Each company mess will have a certified Mess Carver at each end during the meal along with at least 2 cadet recruits.

4th Class Orientation & Training

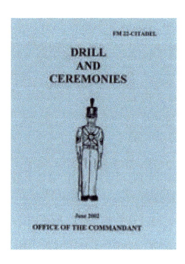

FM 22-CITADEL

DRILL
AND
CEREMONIES

June 2002
OFFICE OF THE COMMANDANT

Though drill instructions have not changed perceptibly over nearly two centuries, the idea of formal meals with a mess carver wanes. The meal system has added the benefit of two meal shifts and even a buffet function. Coward Hall (the cadets' campus mess facility) has undergone several iterations to better serve the Cadet Corps.

 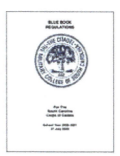 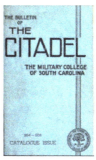 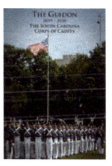

The *Citadel Blue Book* is not the only form of regulations and instruction one would find in the cadet experience. A new *"The Guidon"* is published annually.

Other memoranda are dispensed by the tactical command officers in Jenkins Hall (the Cadet ROTC building). Often, the memos cite what is already published—or re-worded for clarity—as part of the Cadet Blue Book. That Blue Book is much like the Constitution of the United States. It is the base document of the college's command and operations.

Campus communication – between the key factions like the administration, the commandant's office, the academic departments, cadet activities, the Corps of Cadets, Citadel Athletics, the Board of Visitors, The Citadel Alumni Association, and The Citadel Foundation – had an earlier propensity to kill a forest. Electronic means have replaced much of the printed correspondence and has made much of the inter-campus communication instantaneous.

*The Holliday Alumni Center houses The Citadel Alumni Association,*
*The Citadel Foundation,*
*and The Citadel Brigadier Foundation.*

# *Ranking Rank*

You or others you know may have gotten a little overwrought in the hierarchal system that quantified just four years of your life. Fret not. Cadet rank has zero repercussions to a career. None. Nada. Cadet rank could be the most overblown part of the cadet experience. GPA trumps rank. Lifelong friendships trump rank. Graduation trumps rank.

Potential employers are not likely to understand a Citadel graduate's rank in the Corps. They are more likely interested in a graduate's academic standing and extracurricular involvement.

*"They have to pick me.*
*Look how straight I can hold this broom and my GPA*
*is up near two-oh."*
*From the Mind of Ray Mayer.*

In a military environment, it is essential to establish a chain of command and a sense of responsibility for every cadet. Rank accomplishes these tasks effectively. Citadel cadets range from a three-diamond regimental commander to the simple company-insignia shirt collar of a senior class private. They each have their responsibilities and roles within the Corps of Cadets. First and foremost, they must perform well in the classroom. The rank system requires much extra effort on the part of those chosen for specific purposes by the arbitration of a Jenkins Hall panel to perform organizational tasks. It has to be that way. Those not granted rank still have cadet responsibilities and the much-regimented routines of their fellow cadets. In so many ways, the cadets without rank have heightened skills that will enable them to flourish in their careers to the same extent that graduate rank holders will.

*Rank boards…or "This is Your Life."*
*From the Mind of Ray Mayer.*

In the years beyond the diploma, the "rank of life" becomes those who have better utilized their Citadel experience. These graduates may or may not have been the people of the epaulets. They may or may not have been Summerall Guards or among the "Who's Who of Colleges and Universities." They all graduated with dissimilar experiences in a common foundation of training. A cadet entrusted with rank has a jump on some benefits of the cadet experience, but he or she would be wise to recognize the larger value of the ring that bears the same number as his or her classmate.

By example, many cadets who went on to command life after graduation as senior privates exist. Every cadet should become familiar with two that stand out.

*Lt. General John W. Rosa, Jr.*
*The Citadel Class of 1973*

**John W. Rosa, Jr.**, graduated as a senior private in 1973. Rosa was a football scholarship athlete with an outstanding academic record. After sustaining a debilitating knee injury as the team's starting quarterback at spring practice late in his sophomore year, Rosa turned his attention to other career goals. Prior to his junior year, he accepted a contract to join the United States Air Force. After earning his commission on graduation day, Rosa began an impressive career as an Air Force pilot. He rose in both rank and stature. He logged 3,600 flying hours in the A-7, A-10, the Hunter and Jaguar aircraft, F-16, F-117A, HH-60G, and HC-130[14] prior to his emergence into top USAF administrative capacities, including as military spokesperson for the Pentagon after the September 11, 2001, terrorist attacks. Prior to serving as The Citadel's 19th president, General Rosa served as the Superintendent of the United States Air Force Academy in Colorado Springs, Colorado. His impact upon the cadets at the Air Force Academy—and upon Citadel cadets as a twelve-year president of The Citadel—is inestimable.

*Entrepreneur L. William Krause, Citadel Class of 1963.*

**L. William Krause** graduated in 1963 as a senior private. An electrical engineering major, Krause moved to California to begin a career in technologies. His meteoric rise through various leadership roles with Hewlett-Packard underscored his sense of product engineering and market demand. By 1987 he became the chairman of the board of 3COM, a split subsidiary of the giant HP parent company. After retiring in 1993, Krause started his own venture capital firm, LWK Ventures. He has served on boards and in myriad guiding capacities of other large IT firms while expanding his influence across the burgeoning technologies industry. He and his wife Gay initiated the Krause Center for Leadership and Ethics at The Citadel with three gifts totaling well north of $10 million. His view?

"Why not give back to the institution that supplied you with the foundation for a life of success?" Krause stated. "And if, as a senior private, I can do it, why not you?"[15]

Conversely, there are many stories of the predicted success of the high-ranking echelon of cadets. Gaining rank in the Corps of Cadets is not a predictor, nor a guarantee of future accomplishment. It is simply a measure of responsibility conferred upon young people, generally aged 19 to 21, based on their composite adaptation to the rigors of Citadel life at that stage of their development. Is having rank better than not having rank? Perhaps. In each case, that would be a matter of the individual cadet's own assessment and personal development.

*"I have prime overnight delivery.*
*I can start being slack right away."*
**From the Mind of Ray Mayer.**

Rank is a fine goal, and it is part of the system that develops leadership. But it is not the be-all and end-all of the cadet experience. It is the post-graduation realities of life that determine a former cadet's rise in prominence and stature. A Citadel diploma has no notation in its script to signify a cadet's military standing in the Corps. Potential employers look for the degree, not the chevrons.

# The Humor of It All

If a graduate spent his or her time taking The Citadel too seriously, a jumbo jet full of humorous opportunities would have been missed. There is no humor like cadet humor. It is unique. One best witnesses this idiosyncrasy at a class reunion, when spouses are utterly puzzled over what classmates find hilarious.

Some of the humor is timeless, yet some has timed out by the changing times.

We are all familiar with "love-hate relationships," but The Citadel embodies the inverse of that connection. More likely, the cadet experience becomes a "hate-love relationship." Universally, cadets report the misery of being there and the exaltation of what that misery became. The commonalities of the experience bring every cadet together to enjoy the irony, the satire, and the pranks. Those smiling remembrances seem never to age.

Buildings were nicknamed for their humor purpose. Every cadet recognizes Jenkins Hall as "the Toolshed" and the football stadium as "the Boneyard." As an aside, dozens of human remains were excavated from Johnson Hagood Stadium during its 2006-2007 revitalization. Yet the "Boneyard" name predated those discoveries because city records showed there was once a potter's field at the stadium site. When the machinery arrived and remains were discovered, the field truly became "the Boneyard." A "potter's field" is the common term in cities for the burial site of paupers and those unknown and unclaimed at the time of death. Our stadium was, in fact, a potter's field. At times, the noise levels could wake up the dead.

Terse names for the mess hall seem to become more descriptive with each generation of cadets. Coward Hall, the cadet dining facility, has had more nicknames that any other. It has been variously called Mystery Meat Theater, the Rat Farm, and the Ward of the Flies. Other monikers are less flowery and less suitable for print.

*The broad deliverance promenade to Coward Hall, The Citadel dining facility named for Colonel Asbury Coward, Class of 1854, who served as Citadel Superintendent from 1890 to 1908.*

All buildings on campus, at one time or another, were reduced to cadet nicknames that described them much better

than their historic names.  Naming academic buildings became its own sport.  Because the Daniel Library was one of
the few buildings of the 1970s that had central air conditioning (to provide humidity-protection for the books and por-
traits), it gained acceptance across campus as "Nap Haven."
Well, libraries are quiet.  There were well-placed study tables
on the second floor that cadets would jostle to claim between
classes.  The best location on campus for "shut eye" is the
college library—and that fact escapes no one's sense of irony.
In more recent years, the air conditioning inside Summerall
Chapel has overtaken the library by the added feature of more
available seating.  That's not to say that some of those drowsy
cadets are not at prayer! Traditions of culture-acclimation
transcend each era.

It was in Coward Hall where most of the non-Southern-cul-
tured knobs were first introduced to grits.  Many had no idea
how to prepare grits for consumption, prompting many a mess
carver's suggestions of ketchup or mustard.  Upperclassmen
stared, sternly amused, as many grits-uninitiated knobs took
advice to try grits as a sandwich spread with peanut butter.

At various times the blandness of the food would—by its
listless distribution—initiate the most legendary and destructive of the campus calamities—a food fight.  Cadets found
that food fights were better with pork chops than with fried
chicken by the sheer improved aerodynamics that pork chops
presented.  Nothing compared with the wider impact than
a bowl of gravy.  Pork chops were bullets.  Gravy was the
grenade.

Commiserating became a cadet sport.  This was especially seen when tours were walked on the "quad."  There is no

punishment recorded outside the cadet sallyports quite like marching for fifty minutes while sporting an out-of-service World War I level Army rifle missing its firing pin. Hardened criminals painting license plates have it better. Tours are meant as a physical deterrent. Yet cadet graduates seem to laugh more about the circumstance of walking tours than any other experience. It is a colossal waste of time and serves no purpose in any academic sense. As graduates, the "badge" of walking tours supersedes the void of the experience for those who escaped this disciplinary action.

In so many cases, the people who laugh about walking tours are laughing about the tour punishments of others—not their own. The misery of others allows no place for sympathy and elevates the salting of extraordinary humor. It's a cadet thing, and that attitude helps graduates deal with the misfortunes of life beyond.

Usually, the inter-cadet humor reaches its most irreverent level in the devious use of uncommon phraseology. Unique phraseology exalts nearly every cadet descriptive. One would suspect that these accepted "in-barracks terms" are harvested by the wide footprint of communities from which the cadets arrive on campus. Often, the way a cadet phrases an insult or command only makes sense inside the sallyports. These descriptives become their own cultural language. The acronyms foster even further insulation of the exchanges.

*"Hey dude, this is the food court. Relax."*
**From the Mind of Ray Mayer.**

"Hey crud-waste, did that smack-wad Johnson go XMD and leave his CG post during ESP?"

That's a proper cadet question understood Corps-wide. The colorful language is as much a part of the campus culture as the universal lament of dress parades on Friday afternoons.

For the uninitiated, the egos of those latent high school campus stars are adjusted vehemently during that first intense week of training as a "knob." The "knob" terminology arose from the similarity of a doorknob after an incoming cadet's first haircut—also called a "buzz cut." The talent of the barber becomes inconsequential as all of the incoming cadet's hair is sheered like the commercial process of a New Zealand shepherd's flock. The initial female haircuts are different, yet still in the indiscriminate style of submission to the daunting plebe system. The recollection of those first days—especially the haircuts—never fails to amuse.

The sideburns and summer-cropped mustaches disappear, as well. The adage is that you have to want to be at The Citadel because any other circumstance will likely result in an early departure.

There is other levity in those first few weeks that goes un-acknowledged—by the freshman class as well as the cadre. This is the period when *time management*, *capacity*, *physical conditioning*, and *endurance* are tested.

The naïveté of an incoming freshman class breeds its own brand of humor—especially those who are not familiar with this region of the country. It's an annual right-of-passage. Local visitors in the know come to see the new cadets report as free entertainment each August.

The cadre descends.

*"Hey Mr. Howard, can you get some of your company knob volunteers together to take down the campus summer moss and put up the winter moss this weekend?"*

*At The Citadel, we know such terms as the "Rack Monster."*
*Elsewhere, these are known as sleep endorphins.*
*From the Mind of Ray Mayer.*

Advice from cadre or upperclassmen returnees is taken as serious direction.

*"I remember my first leave. Cadets get in free at all College of Charleston fraternity and sorority parties. It's easy. Just show up."*

*"The biology department needs specimens and will pay for live palmetto bugs. I catch 'em with my field cap rain cover. Bring them to the department head. He gives extra credit."*

*"Our company football players like that new performance band, Furman. Make sure that they know that you like Furman, too."*

Knobs beware! There's another wave of shenanigans likely to come from returning senior privates just after Knob Week.

*"Next Wednesday is national fried chicken day here in Charleston. You're allowed to order the family picnic bucket for your classmates during ESP. Just have it delivered by Uber Eats to the front sallyport."*

*"Saturday afternoon leave is fabulous. Check out the horse barn on Anson Street and ask for free chips."*

*"When it's raining you can cut across the parade ground. If somebody yells something to you, just keep going. Some just don't read the memos."*

Even the cadet newspaper, *The Brigadier*, chimed in. The satire of Pat Day, '73, as the first Scarlet Pimpernel and Gordon Bell, '74, as Steven T. Fhour in *Fhourmations* presented a humorous inside look at the Corps of Cadets. Both writers remained anonymous in their roles—Day being pursued by red-faced tactical officers, and Bell being pursued by irate upperclassmen cadets. The deceptive Bell had them searching the wrong company looking for "Knob Fhour!"

*Just another TAC attack.*
*"Write him up, son. I'll confiscate the evidence."*
*From the Mind of Ray Mayer.*

*The Brigadier* became the home of the finest cartoonist in anyone's memory in the person of Ray Mayer, '74, whose "rack monsters" and "football jocks" became fearsome caricatures. His artful heading for the sports editor's column "In the Doghouse" lasted several decades.

There was a definitive sense of "freedom of speech" unmasked, even at a military college. The college's literary magazine, *The Shako*, was fair game. As an aside, the annual humor award ($25) came from a ditty written by this book's author in 1973. I had taken an elective course in astronomy because I was sky-fascinated like the Mayans and the Druids. But the coursework presented by a professor named Berne was mechanical, dry, and boring. Taking the course was a colossal mistake. So, I expressed myself.

## *A Sojourn Through Berne*
### *-or-*
## *There Are Just So Many Things You Can Tell a Scope*

*Gracious macious spacious bard—*
*Your astronomy course is mighty hard.*
*You've eclipsed the class in meetings helt,*
*And I still can't find Orion's Belt.*
*The Zenith, Centaurus, the celestial sphere—*
*Hello Cassiopeia, is Cygnus there?*
*And what's that about the Ursas Two?*
*The entire universe curses you!*
*The radius of Mercury is a fact*
*That you should teach with much more tact*
*Will a Doppler shift into galactic cluster?*
*How much trivia must I muster?*
*You say "Be objective when speaking of stars*
*Or refracting the rectilinear propagation of Mars."*
*The terms you use, imbued with malice,*
*In Time ephemeris and Aurora Borealis.*
*Virgo. Libra, Pisces, Aquarius—*
*Are you Taurus or Leo Sagittarius?*
*I'd distinguish solar from sidereal day—*
*If those nebulae weren't in the Milky Way.*
*Life is not a bowl of cherries*
*And neither are your heavenly queries.*
*The astronomical knowledge I've tried to nurse*
*Is surrendered lightly in this verse.*
*March 23, 1973*

As always, the professor won. I received a dismal "C" for my efforts but did humor the others in the class who felt as I did. I won the award again in 1974 with, "It Was the Satirists Who Made Achilles a Heel." I received an "A" in that course.

As in real life, humor makes all offerings digestible.

The famed "Furman Five" created their own brand of mischief. Suffering through a difficult football season, a post-evening-mess pep rally drew only fifty cadets. Five of them saw the need for an injection of *"Esprit de Corps"* in November of 1973. It had been ten years since an earlier Furman raid resulted in cadets kidnapping the Furman Paladin horse, its mascot. The horse was returned safely.

The 1973 Furman raid was expeditiously planned as a spray-painting mission to the Furman campus—more than 200 miles away—that evening! The five cadets carefully escaped the campus undetected, knowing that the AWOL offense would have them walking forty tours and serving confinements to the campus until the punishment was completed. They made it to Furman by midnight and used up ten cans of light blue and white spray paint in places that would be highly noticeable in daylight. They succeeded in using up all ten cans (two cans apiece) over the next hour. The senior cadets deftly escaped the gated Furman campus and returned to The Citadel just before the first bugle of morning formation.

The Citadel upset our biggest rival, Furman University, that Saturday, 26-21. It was our third and final victory of the dismal 3-8 season. Eventually the Furman Five turned themselves in, took up a Corps-wide collection to pay for the Furman paint damage, and began walking tours. Fatefully, a rare amnesty event occurred when Vice President Gerald Ford visited the campus. They had walked only two tours each. The experience exceeded the repercussions. The Furman Five became legend.

Overnight missions were not limited to painting Furman's campus. But it was those trips that were almost always exposed by both the *Greenville News* and the Charleston *News & Courier* (now *Post & Courier*). Cadets will be cadets.

Other inside-the-campus calamities arose. The Citadel Infirmary and the cadet laundry had their own legacies. Nearly every cadet who ever spent their academic career at The Citadel has these two things in common. They have been shorted by the laundry and they have been stuck in the infirmary. These are part of the lore that is not actually lore. The laundry loses clothing items at a pace that may indicate an underworld scheme to clothe a small country in Latin America. It was like the forced air tube at a bank drive-in. The laundry went in, and like the quick sound of the air vacuum, they were gone forever, never to be returned.

*The Cadet Laundry: Where more than just socks are apt to mysteriously disappear.*

A cadet knows to avoid the infirmary unless dire medical treatment is the only option remaining. By reporting, classmates will deride you, the upper classes will scold you, and the professors will hold it against you. Yet the worst of it is that the infirmary will overreact to everything as if their staff is responsible for keeping the bubonic plague in check. The Citadel Infirmary is the most uncomfortable place to be sick in all of America. A common cold that requires antibiotics could detain a cadet for a solid week—or until the antibiotics run out. In effect, The Citadel Infirmary is the most dreaded building on campus—even surpassing the ultra-military Jenkins Hall or the "House of Vacant Cuisine," Coward Hall. Nearly every graduate has a story about a simple visit that turned into a crisis at the Infirmary.

*"I reported last Thursday after mess and got out on Tuesday. It turns out that what I had was indigestion. Well, it was just after I left the mess hall."*

*"XMD, sir! Ingrown toenail, sir. No sir, not fatal. Unless you consider the option of suicide in lieu of returning to the plebe system, sir!"*

*The Mary Bennett Murray Infirmary at The Citadel could
be termed both famous and infamous.
The designation is determined from which side
of the front door one stands.
To be excused military duty (XMD) for medical reasons
can become a difficult status to overcome.*

The routine humor of the cadet life is ingrained. It comes from weekend ROTC expedition requirements, the timing of general amnesty orders, the mixture of campus uniforms during intermittent rain showers, classmates getting "busted," a particularly awful parade performance grade or SMI inspection, or a "Dear John" letter posted on the company bulletin board. These things do not happen on other campuses. A cadet is at the center of a comedic black hole. It sucks everything and everyone into the grinning darkness for light years beyond.

Some humor exceeds what one would expect from polite society. "Gross" is a common term in cadet life that has no superlatives. There's no grosser or grossest. Perhaps brought into common cadet parlance through *Blue Book* infractions such as "gross personal appearance" and "gross poor judgment," the term "Gross" is seen daily to evoke yet more Corps experiences in inside-the-gates humor. A passerby would not understand what makes a cadet bellow in laughter. "Gross" has its own category.

"Gross" exists and grows on the campus like mildew on the shady side of Bond Hall.

*There was the story of a junior cadet who had a large shoulder boil that kept growing. He saw it as an income opportunity and charged a quarter to gather a reasonably large crowd after ESP to have it lanced by his roommate. "Gross out" events were not limited to lancing boils. The Bond Volunteers enjoyed a standard of their own.*

The *coup de grâce* for every class occurs on graduation day. It is at this full-dress formal event that a somewhat random cadet speaker closes out the four-year journey. This speaker is accorded the largest cheer of the day. Typically, his or her last name begins with the letter "Z" as the last graduate of the class. Tradition holds that this cadet gives insightful and mostly humorous remarks to summarize four years of perspective. These speakers usually evoke the greatest class response. They own this privilege of the moment simply by alphabetical circumstance.

*The large Citadel Ring monument is the focal*
*point of those who enter Lesesne Gate.*

*The year designation changes with each senior class.*

It's an inordinate construct of time that the four years in the cadet Corps can dominate a lifetime of humorous memories in a ratio that makes no sense to anyone—other than in the memories of other Citadel graduates. When it is considered that cadet humor only existed for four years of a cadet experience and yet dominates a lifetime of robust laughter, it makes The Citadel all-the-more unique.

# Section Two:
# The Consequence of Character

Let's talk more about the template that comes with the diploma. We've called it the ***toolbox*** because at any point one could reach in and find just the right tool for every situation. Carrying the toolbox forward, there will be times when pliers are the best choice, but the user opts for a hammer. The craftsman has to make decisions—does a situation require ingenuity, duty, or compassion? Discerning the right tools at the correct timing becomes a talent borne of experience. It's good to know that the tools are available, but it may take some trial and error to know which tool and what timing to select.

The following chapters are meant to rediscover the tools that are part of the four-year experience. These tools can be developed well outside of The Citadel by those who pursue a well-rounded life. The endorsement of what is provided intensely at The Citadel works well within the guideline of life's comportment. No one is perfect, but everyone has a sense of perfection. In that regard, The Citadel lends a captivating experience that keeps cadets in focus for a time certain.

And then you graduate.

## The Next Part of Life

You're in demand! There's either a *demand* to show up at a military base somewhere because you contracted to do so, or you may have already established your next career move. You may be inclined to further your education through a graduate program, medical school, or law school. Or you may be among the "free agents" who are weighing options to begin a career in any number of positive avenues.

Your academic major likely has an impact. For instance, The Citadel's wide array of engineering programs has met high annual public demand. Other programs adapt—such as criminal justice, cybersecurity, sports management, and nursing.

The president, the provost, and the commandant—along with the Board of Visitors—carefully assess the career opportunities of the future. The Citadel has been adept at adjusting the curriculum to meet the public need. This endeavor has become the science of predictive analysis. An institution that prides itself on principled and ethical leadership adds the specter of an ever-changing world as a component of its preparation.

As an alumnus, it is presumed that every graduate will join The Citadel Alumni Association (CAA). Why should you? Once a grad is on the other side of Lesesne Gate, the CAA is "command central" of everything Citadel. Think of the Association as your best and wisest friend. They can locate alumni in remote regions or in the large metropolitan areas you may travel. Because of the college's appeal to international students and our graduate contributions to the military, there is a Citadel presence nearly everywhere on the globe. The Citadel Alumni Association keeps tabs.

Join. It's your umbilical cord connecting you to the lifeblood of your future. The CAA places its importance within a structured purpose:

*The Association is organized and shall operate a supporting organization exclusively for the benefit of, to perform the functions of, and to carry out the purposes of The Citadel, the Military College of South Carolina ("The Citadel"). To this end, the objectives of the Association shall include the following:*

1. *To provide a private, self-sustaining, non-profit organization to support, advance and promote the ideals and purposes of The Citadel, the Military College of South Carolina, the Corps of Cadets, and the Alumni;*

2. *To foster, perpetuate, and preserve the history, memories, values, and traditions of The Citadel, the Military College of South Carolina, the Corps of Cadets, and the Alumni; and*

3. *To sell, award, and determine the right to wear the ring of The Citadel, which ring and the trademark thereto are owned by the Association.*[16]

You likely knew that your ring was developed and authorized by the CAA. That's precisely why the president of The Citadel Alumni Association has a role in graduation to allow the cadet-graduate to turn the ring around with the class number facing outward.  The Classes of '99 and '66 could be confused…but not likely.  Those in the Class of 2000 never need to pay attention to the direction of their rings.  The ring that reads "00" has to be considered an artful boast.  U.S. House of Representatives member Nancy Mace has one.

In essence, the CAA connects people.  The Association can be helpful in connecting careers, as well.  Think of the CAA as the cruise ship and you as a dinghy drifting in uncharted waters.  The cruise ship throws you a tow line to get you to a lively port where so many other dinghies have been moored.  Come to think of it, that's a dinghy way to put it.

The Citadel has a Doctoral degree in events!

*The 2008 Renovation (rebuilding) of the iconic Johnson Hagood Stadium was a four year alumni effort chaired by the author.*
*Photo by author.*

When the renovation of Johnson Hagood Stadium was completed in 2008, the then-Athletic Director Les Robinson likened the achievement to remodeling the college's front porch. It's true that the stadium often gives visitors their first impression of The Citadel. But the stadium serves a much larger function. It houses the largest gatherings of Citadel alumni year-by-year. Grads return to perhaps as many as six home football games each year. They have bought the suites and club seats along with PSLs—private seat licenses. Season tickets are in order. They are there to rekindle friendships and enjoy experiences beyond NCAA football. The new Sansom Field had artificial turf installed in 2020. The new video scoreboard (fall of 2021) became an impressive addition, along with the Altman Center (meeting space and new locker room facilities).

Regardless of the football team's won-loss record, The Citadel routinely attracts more fans than any other Southern Conference team. That dynamic is rooted in The Citadel cadet experience. Alumni bring their families for other reasons than football. And the football is usually entertaining. The highlight of every season is Homecoming weekend, when classes return in levels of anniversary years divided by five. These weekends usually culminate a class-oriented reunion giving campaign with halftime check presentations to The Citadel Foundation often topping seven-figures.

*"Being a senior private is like being a king. More bubbly, Chauncey!"*
*From the Mind of Ray Mayer.*

Since 2005, another organization has arisen to support events. The Citadel StrayDog Society has its own football game tailgate tent for graduates, friends, and family to enjoy. It reached well outside of the alumni base and hosts the annual StrayDog Homecoming Jamboree—a sellout each year. The Homecoming Jamboree is mindful of a senior class party—on steroids. It's the best alumni party offered each and every year. The StrayDogs feature other alumni gathering events year-round as a catalyst for good times.

The Citadel Foundation has its own brand of celebrations—often related to the completion of a capital campaign.

These are usually held in a memorable fashion that elevates the case for support shared by all. Think "first class."

The Athletics programs and support organizations have developed a following as well. There is The Citadel Football Association, Diamond Dogs Club (baseball), The Citadel Wrestling Association, and The Citadel Basketball Association that replaced an earlier Citadel Fastbreak Club (established in 1984). Alumni who are so inclined may join as they wish. However, one does not have to be a graduate to join! Support also comes from parents and friends, as well as corporate entities and community members.

In that vein, the grandaddy organization for the support of Citadel athletics is The Citadel Brigadier Foundation, Inc. This is the organization that provides athletic scholarships for cadet-student-athletes across our eleven NCAA sports. Women's sports include Cross Country, Golf, Soccer, Rifle, Track & Field, and Volleyball. Men's sports are Baseball, Basketball, Tennis, Football, Wrestling, Cross Country, Track & Field, and Rifle. Rifle is a coeducational sport. The Citadel Brigadier Foundation (TCBF) supports athletic scholarships for over 350 student-athletes each year. TCBF memberships afford privileges of preferred athletic parking and seating. The benefit of supporting Citadel athletics assists the college in recruiting and competing at all levels of athletic endeavor.

TCBF hosts several functions each year, most notably The Citadel Kickoff Classic. This golf tournament is held each August, hosting alumni and Citadel friends on two to three golf courses. This is the best annual participation event on the college calendar and has raised nearly $2 million for The Citadel Brigadier Foundation since its inception.

*The Citadel StrayDog Jamboree attracts returning*
*Homecoming classes.*
*Photo by author.*

The Citadel has an Athletic Hall of Fame. Each year the CAHOF inducts five or six outstanding ladies and gentlemen as athletes and honorary members. The annual evening banquet sells out and is considered the most entertaining of The Citadel's impressive list of annual events. The Citadel Athletic Hall of Fame has extensive displays in McAlister Fieldhouse. A benefactor, the late Gene Moore, '53, provided considerable funds for the development of a unique setting within the campus for a new stand-alone exhibit space.

Other parts of The Citadel's extensive reach include annual events to induct high-level leaders into the college's academic ranks of achievement. The most notable of these is the Tommy & Victoria Baker School of Business Hall of Fame. Its list champions those lauded across the nation within the myriad aspects of industry, finance, business, and politics. Prepare to be impressed. The Zucker Family School of Education and The Citadel School of Engineering foster similar venues to celebrate educators and engineers across the community, respectively. The Citadel Graduate College has positioned itself to become a regional leader in the facilitation of post-graduate degrees in education and other disciplines. The Citadel produces outstanding teachers.

Even the Daniel Library has its own following. The Friends of the Daniel Library holds several annual events with artists, authors, and people of some heightened fascination. These are evening events throughout the academic year that are generally free to the public. This society has a nominal annual membership, and their events are meant to cement academic and cultural relationships across the Charleston community.

The Citadel Graduate College (CGC) has its own niche and is quite active in campus events. The CGC offers over sixty graduate degrees. The foresight to offer wide and current graduate disciplines has been a catalyst in the *U.S. News & World Report* rankings. They list The Citadel as the perennial number one *best value* in Southern colleges and universities among those offering up to a master's degree. We're a great college...and we're an even better deal!

As a graduate, one becomes intrinsically connected to The Citadel by taking advantage of joining alumni groups. The physical proximity of the graduate's home, if distanced, should pose little loss of participation. Being a graduate offers so much more once a commitment is made to engage.

# *Capacity*

In the **Foreword,** several life tools of the cadet graduate were divulged. Many of these are ingrained into every cadet and should be further explored. **Capacity** is often overlooked, but essential to the make-up of a cadet graduate.

Have you ever been in an athletic training facility while pursuing a physical goal? It may be that you wanted to run a 5K race, or bike away calories, or lift weights to build core muscles. It's not easy to get started and, in fact, it's really easy to quit. But if you stick with a routine, you build *capacity*. There are mornings when it's too cold or rainy to get to the gym. There are windy days and other seasons when the humidity is just too hot to get out and jog. But dedicated people persevere in order to build capacity.

One of my favorite tongue-in-cheek movie lines comes from *The Outlaw Josey Wales.* "Vow to endeavor to persevere" is a line spoken by Chief Dan George, who played the role of a Cherokee chief in the movie. When goals are set, there are obstacles that must be met. That's why successful people "vow to endeavor to persevere."

In the gym, it is a matter of finding capacity and training your body to overcome the immediate sacrifice of exertion. At The Citadel, exertion is part of the daily routine. The process produces results. Each cadet will approach capacity in order to measure resolve.

What is capacity? Is everyone's capacity the same? Do we approach one capacity only to see it grow to another level? Capacity, then, is a measurement.

It seems that physical records from yesteryear are mostly forgotten because of the constant assault on new world records by modern athletes with new training regimens. Tedious methods developed by analytics and technologies have improved diets. Capacity has advanced. For instance, in 1891, the world 100-meter sprint record was 10.8 seconds.[17] That record has been broken—progressively—27 times over the next 130 years. Usain Bolt from Jamaica holds the current world record, set in 2009 at 9.572 seconds.[18] All track and field events have unilaterally improved by the same formula—regimen, method, and diet. The world record for completing a marathon (26.2 miles) was two hours and fifty-five minutes in 1908. In 2018, Eliud Kipchoge of Kenya set the new marathon record at 2:01:39.[19] Think about that. In a century, the marathon record was reduced by nearly an hour—or a third of the time lopped off! Humanity has become bigger, faster, and stronger in every sense.

*"I know it's four a.m.*
*But my squad corporal said these shoes need work."*
*From the Mind of Ray Mayer.*

One could certainly postulate a century ago that these track records would be considered inhuman. What about a century from now? It is a certainty that both the sprint and marathon records will be broken. Why? We are designed to produce more capacity.

The human brain has unused capacity, too. Every professor at The Citadel may have found me to be contemptuous in that regard. But the myth that we only use a low percentage has been debunked many times. Neurologists and neurosurgeons are learning more about our "hard drive" in their own progression. We use all of our brain but not all of our brain's capacity. We learn daily. The human brain has astonishing abilities and even recuperative powers. I know this personally.

I've had two brain surgeries. *After* the second surgery, I authored three books in ten months!

We cannot limit our capacity. We had no idea what it was as a cadet. We will continue to explore our horizons as we journey through life.

There are other non-measured capacities.

What about emotional intelligence and human interaction capacities? The maturation process during our four years in a restrictive environment allows us to enhance these other capacities. In a publication by Steven Brunkhorst, these common human characteristics are defined as capacities.

1. *Helping someone in his or her time of tragedy or need shows the capacity for human goodness.*

2. *Listening closely to another's words and experience shows the capacity for soulful communication.*

3. *Understanding the pain, sorrow, or loss of another person shows the capacity for empathy.*

4. *Believing the best about others, and offering time, support, and friendship show the capacity for trust.*

5. *Apologizing for a past mistake shows the capacity for strong character and trustworthiness.*

6. *Forgiving the errors of a fellow human being shows the capacity to receive forgiveness.*

7. *Supporting the truth, even when it is unpopular, shows the capacity for honesty and integrity.*

8. *Compromising when it is best for the welfare of others shows the capacity for teamwork.*

9. *Giving time and effort to assist others to be successful shows the capacity for sincerity.*

10. *Being curious about life, its people, and its mysteries shows the capacity for learning.*

11. *Praying for the welfare of family, friends, and all of humanity shows the capacity for love.*

12. *Waiting for God's answer to a prayer shows the capacity for faith and patience.*

13. *Accepting the answer to a prayer, whatever it might be, discovering its blessings, and then moving on shows the capacity for gratitude.*

14. *Believing in a God-given purpose throughout long and difficult seasons of scarcity shows the capacity for determination and hope.*

15. *Taking risks, making mistakes, and learning from all experiences show the capacity for being human.*

16. *Getting up after having fallen down or suffered failure shows the capacity for resolve.*

17. *Persisting resolutely to navigate life's rapids, scale its mountains, move beyond its perceived limitations, and arrive at its finish line with faith and dignity shows the capacity for achievement.*[20]

In essence, the growth of our capacities—physical, mental, and emotional—rounds out our character and our experience as humans. We are constantly discovering more about ourselves. And concurrently, we find out much more about the character of others. In so many cases, these others are classmates from our four years at The Citadel. It is not unusual to find that classmates hardly known at "El Cid" emerge to become the closest of friends by the simple connection of the year designated on The Citadel ring. These contemporaries grow into life together.

Capacity is an endearing and romantic notion in the sense that we start somewhere in a direction where we plan to ameliorate our own life. That journey to expand our capacity is the verve and sustenance of living.

# Adherence to Duty

Every battalion at The Citadel has the same plaque in the main sallyport. It features a quotation from Confederate General Robert E. Lee.

*"Duty is the sublimest word in the English language."* With deference to the correct superlative of the word *sublime*—to mean inspiring, exalted, or uplifting—General Lee finished that thought in a slightly different letter to his son George Washington Custis Lee on April 5, 1852. The letter was sent just a few years after Lee's role in the Mexican War (1848) where, as a captain, he positioned cannons for the siege of Vera Cruz.[21]

*"Duty, then, is the sublimest word in our language. Do your duty in all things like the old Puritan. You cannot do more, you should never wish to do less."*

*This often-polished brass plaque can be seen in the entry sallyport of each battalion.*
*Photo by author.*

"Most sublime" would have been correct. And there have been some challenges to the authenticity of the letter from which the statement derives. But let's not nitpick. The

66

sentiment is that we rise to the sense of duty, and the sentiment remains true. Duty defines our character and our commitment. It is duty that transcends all else, especially in the military. Yet duty reaches into every phase of the human character. Is it not *duty* to be a provider when inclement weather would otherwise thwart that requirement in an outdoor-career responsibility? Is it not *duty* (and love) to take care of aging parents despite the inconvenience and time commitment? Is it not *duty* to stand up for one's convictions despite formidable opposition?

Citadel cadets understand duty. And then duty becomes part of the character of a lifetime of service to others—family, religious affiliations, community concerns, friends, and even the country at large.

There may be nothing quite as chivalric as duty. Duty, like chivalry, requires readiness, courage, strength of character, and honor. Yet the sense of duty is not as common as one might believe.

*"Son, I know you're studying and have a 3.9,
but you need to understand what's really important."
**From the Mind of Ray Mayer.***

Duty has significant cultural obligations. For instance, in a world that seems to suppress the importance of dual-parenting in the life of children, it seems that single-parent causes are celebrated. While the vigilance and sacrifice of a single parent show inestimable courage, there is no doubt that the benefit derived by children from married and loving parents proves more the effective means. Situations can require the former. But dual parenting spreads the duty of childrearing to a team effort. Besides social enhancements, the obvious benefit of a two-parent household is that it reduces the poverty rate substantially. Sadly, poverty rates have a direct impact upon the education, well-being, and expectations of children. While it may not be a duty to continue a failing relationship or marriage, there is an inherent duty to remain intrinsically involved in the lives of children produced within a marriage. According to a report in the *Washington Post,*

> *We know that children raised by two parents — at school, in the future labor market, in their own marriages — [are more advantaged] than children raised by a single mom or dad. And from this fact, it might seem easy to conclude that marriage wields some outsized power over a child's life — that its absence creates unstable homes and chaotic families, while its presence nurtures them.[22]*

Perhaps as a society we underestimate the "duty" to marry well. Should this not be the case, the emphasis concerning children of a marriage should justly be to parent well. Duties extend to formal relationships as well as to those less contractual.

There is also a provider duty imposed upon working-force adults. At a minimum, it is a *duty* to be self-reliant; that is, to provide for oneself. In theory, parents did this for children within a time certain. They provide a home environment, safety, nourishment, mentorship, and education. Once the child completes his or her education, the responsibility changes because the assumption is that a young lady or young man has gained all of the abilities and confidence to "go it on their own."

A duty is a commitment.

***Graduation Day is a beginning.***
***Photo provided by The Citadel.***

Duty is a far-encompassing concept. There is civic duty that no American can deny or escape. It is part and parcel of living in a democracy:

> *Democracy requires not just obeying the law,*
> *though; it requires that people actively participate*
> *in the political process. This means voting, of course,*
> *but it is usually thought that not just any effort at*
> *voting will suffice—the citizen must stay informed*

*of political affairs and make a rational choice among the options presented to her in the voting booth. Is there a duty to vote, then? And, if so, does this duty require that citizens become sufficiently well-informed about political affairs and relevant facts?[23]*

The answers are "yes" and "yes." It is our duty as citizens to be aware of issues, of political impact, of political candidates and their platforms, and to be able to cast a ballot within those core beliefs and ideals. There is a duty to support country—through serving the country and through the voting process.

Duty grows. Beyond relationships, there are duties related to friendships, to community, to career, and to country. Duty may be the most potent seedling of a young cadet graduate moving into a full life of responsibility. It is ingrained into the psyche. It is character on steroids.

Indeed, it is sublime.

# *Time Management*

It's all about time management. You know that life-changing, two-word designation well. From the day a cadet reports, the responsibility of time management rests upon a rigid schedule that has very few flexibilities.

Time management is among the most important personal assets one can master, yet it is noticeably deficient in most of the world today. It is ingrained in the regimented Citadel character. Together with *duty, honor, and respect*, a graduate may guide the earth by its rope handles on a downhill pull.

*"It's high tide and we're missing Cadet Murtaugh."*
*From the Mind of Ray Mayer.*

It is inherent in the "afterlife of barracks living" that graduates become task masters. Typically, even the most daunting tasks are approached with the pragmatic view of what it takes to fully complete. Deft preparation and time management are the twin engines that reduce the complexities of overwhelming assignments.

A cadet schedule would look ridiculous to the "Joe College" student—in contemporary times as well as in the days of yore. There is no time for sunning on Marion Square or throwing the frisbee on the quad with the late-waking fraternity guys down the way. Instead, a cadet schedule includes a classroom overload with up to three weekly graded hours of ROTC. Typically, a cadet takes six 3-hour academic courses per semester. A science lab (engineering, chemistry, biology) requires another hour, and a leadership class demands additional time. There are morning periods of required physical training and afternoon periods of required military drill. There are haircuts and faculty conferences, symposiums, and Greater Issues speakers. Active cadets sign up for extracurricular activities ranging from cadet chorale to community service to intramural sports to any number of cadet clubs and religious activities. The Citadel annually produces the nation's highest percentage participation in intramural activities. There is a Student Success Center for extra tutoring to enhance academic performance. And there are publication teams like *The Brigadier* (cadet newspaper), *The Shako* (literary journal), *The Gold Star Journal* (peer-reviewed academic journal), and *The Sphinx* (college yearbook). A cadet has access to myriad activities beyond their academic pursuits. Only with an acute awareness of time management would these activities be possible. There is a three-hour evening study period (ESP) and a "lights out" requirement to end the days' activities before it all begins again with morning PT and company formations. Cadet meals and general leave are regimented, as well.

The management of a cadet's time bodes well. There is a rhythm and routine of cadet time management that translates to efficient organizational abilities after graduation.

The most difficult indoctrination is as an incoming freshman.

*Freshmen cadets are immersed in intense military training that continues throughout all four years of cadet life. Cadets are also required to complete four years of military training in the ROTC branch of their choice. These experiences arm cadets with the time-management, discipline and teamwork skills necessary to succeed in both military and civilian careers.*[24]

It is the adjustment one undergoes as a freshman that sometimes hits like a sudden cloudburst. In similarity with other institutions, it may be the first time that the student is away on their own. But unlike incoming college students on other campuses, the profound regimentation and traditions of freshman indoctrination at The Citadel is extraordinary. The adjectives might read as harsh, stoic, Spartan, or adversarial. In every instance, the demands upon the freshman cadet's time may seem insurmountable. That adjustment bodes well over a lifetime as those days of seemingly overwrought minutes and hours become a template for future time management orchestrations.

Cadets do not stop being cadets on weekends. Thus, the skills it takes to command time across requirements and resources becomes the basic adjustment needed to flourish at The Citadel. Time management skills would likely not have similar stringency demands after the cadet moves into the life of a graduate. But that experience remains at the ready.

There is an adage that grew out of World War II suggesting the importance of punctuality. "If you're early, you're on time. If you're on time, you're late. If you're late, there is no excuse." Author Eric Jerome Dickey condensed the sentiment succinctly to: "early is on time, on time is late, and late is unacceptable!"

As cadets we knew the "no excuse" reply all too well. In managing time, we must also manage the anticipation of being on time with travel, parking, and even slow elevators. That planning also becomes a lifetime skill. My father, who knew the Great Depression and served in the Pacific with the U.S. Navy in WWII, was routinely forty-five minutes early in his work career. He knew too many good workers who had lost their livelihoods by being cavalier about their time management. His attitude about time management became infectious.

Managing time is also a sign of "good form"—it shows respect for another's time. Simple things like dentist appointments and social events have segmented times. Being punctual and being ready should impel a person to achieve the higher standards expected in life. Managing time is an art form that so many others, in general, do not embrace. It's an indicator that introduces all the facets of good character.

# *A Lifetime of Honor*

Does one noble element of the cadet experience extend to a lifetime that elevates The Citadel graduate highest among others? The cadet honor code stands alone. It is sacrosanct. Many colleges outside of our campus add their academic code of honor to their manuals as "a student found cheating will be assigned a failing grade to the course." The repercussions are toothless and understandably corrupt the larger academic mission.

The Citadel, in contrast, demands the highest standard possible.

"A cadet does not lie, cheat, or steal, nor tolerate those who do." End of discussion.

There is no ambivalence in the statement. There have been outstanding engineering students, top athletes, and medical school aspirants who have left The Citadel because unassailable evidence determined that a character flaw eliminated their eligibility to continue in an environment of honor.

There is a unique process within the Cadet Honor Code system that merits admiration. The system is adjudicated by the peers of the accused. That is, one who is charged with breaking the tenets of this simply defined honor code has full rights to assemble a defense to be presented to The Citadel Honor Court. These are senior cadets selected by their senior classmates to enforce this most revered attribute of honor. The Cadet Honor Court changes personnel upon each graduation. In essence, the cadets administer the code to the cadets.

***View of Padgett Thomas Barracks to the west***
***from the Daniel Library***
***Photo by author.***

Even the federal military academies do not have the clear stringency of The Citadel's Honor Code. Yet media sources seem to rank colleges on their dearth of honor violations in lieu of the matter of honor itself. An excerpt of explanation about Davidson College's example of personal honesty bears the insight.

> *This school prides itself in the rarity of plagiarism and cheating cases. It's so trusting of the student body that final exams are self-scheduled, so that students can fairly prepare for each test. Examinations are not proctored, and professors usually assign take-home tests. Although this test of trust could be seen as an example of reverse psychology, it seems to be working. The liberal attitude is met with tough*

*sanctions for violations. An unethical move could lead to a $200 fine, community service hours, or indefinite expulsion. At this North Carolina institution, the test of trust is definitely worth passing.*[25]

Davidson College is an outstanding institution of higher education lauded nationally. However, this approach does not particularly monitor the standards of honor. And it hardly penalizes a confirmed lack of honor. They are hardly alone in this regard.

Our media seems to relent when discussing honor as if it were unimportant or a "value added" component separate from the sanctity of the college degree. A *Washington Post* article went as far as calling for the elimination of honor codes in colleges.

*In an age in which collaboration and interpersonal skills are increasingly valued in the workplace, honor codes that rigidly define and punish "cheating" in classrooms have become impractical and antiquated. Campus honor codes have been around nearly as long as higher education in the United States. William & Mary, the second-oldest U.S. college after Harvard (sic), is widely credited with developing the first honor code, in the late 1700s, dictating the standards of ethical conduct for its student body. Since then, roughly 100 colleges have established formal codes setting strict standards on cheating, plagiarism, and other violations of academic integrity. But what constituted "cheating"*

*hundreds of years ago, when exams focused on test-*
*ing knowledge of basic facts, doesn't necessarily ap-*
*ply today. In our modern world, when every known*
*fact is readily accessible on the internet, students are*
*increasingly encouraged to collaborate on projects*
*and share knowledge that inspires creative prob-*
*lem-solving. That kind of teamwork is valued in*
*the working world but is undermined by outdated*
*honor codes.*[26]

The premise above is highly flawed. First of all, honor is part of a person's character, not a collaborative gesture. Through one's honor and personal integrity, a student decides the avenue of his or her academic production outside of the dishonorable avenues of copying, plagiarism, unauthorized collaboration, the posturing of work as his or her own (the lie), and the toleration of others doing the same. When it becomes a group-approved norm to dismiss the "lie," then honor has no more relevance. Thus, honorable people are dishonored.

*"Matriculation" means a commitment to duty, honor,*
*and respect… and a haircut.*
*Photo courtesy The Citadel.*

It is not the intent of this discourse to denigrate other institutions, but rather to extol the importance of the principle of honor ingrained into the life of a cadet graduate. Honor is forever. It is definitive. It is the basis for all actions and reactions in life. And once lost, it is lost forever.

The historical guidepost of honor has diminished across society. Honor, as displayed by cadet graduates, is in short supply and moving southward. Because of social media, dishonor has an anonymous fingerprint. This trend is fast becoming the cultural norm.

*In 1790, 95% of Americans lived in small, rural*
*communities. By the 1990s, 3 out of 4 citizens*

*made their home in urbanized areas. While in small towns everyone can keep track of the doings of their neighbors, in cities and suburbs relationships tend to be more impersonal and anonymous; any city dweller has experienced the sensation of being in a large group of people and yet feeling entirely alone. In large populations you can live out your whole life without anyone checking up on what you're doing, much less judging your reputation as honorable or dishonorable.*

*In cities and smaller towns alike, civic participation and community-mindedness have fallen significantly since WWII. And while honor formerly centered on one's clan, extended families no longer live close together, and familial relations have constricted to the nuclear family alone, which itself is often split up.*

*As a result of these shifts, immoral, unethical, and cowardly behaviors are rarely known outside one's immediate circle of family and friends. And even then, for reasons we'll discuss below, they are more likely to shrug and say, "It's none of my business," or, "To each his own," than to condemn and challenge the errant behavior.*

*The internet has only accelerated the shift towards impersonal and anonymous relationships. Traditional honor is designed to act as a check on*

*people's claims to merit and force them to stand be-*
*hind and defend their insults; exaggerations of one's*
*deeds or shameful actions are called out and chal-*
*lenged by one's associates. On the internet, however,*
*people can claim to be a Navy SEAL or issue the*
*basest of insults to another person without having*
*to prove their claim, suffer consequences for their*
*character, or allow the insulted person to defend*
*themselves. They can be anyone and say anything,*
*all while safely ensconced behind a screen.*[27]

We would not have recognized the avenues in which others could be anonymously dishonored by conjecture or blatant
deviousness. It makes those who carry honor as a badge all
the more welcomed.

Honor is indeed timeless. Honorable people are defined
as such by a society. An infringement upon a person's honor
then becomes a dishonor and, therefore, negates the entire
sense of honor beyond.

The internet and social media have changed the world in
more ways than an information explosion. They have changed
how we rate and assess character.

*Who hasn't sent a text message saying 'I'm on my way'*
*when it wasn't true or fudged the truth a touch in their*
*online dating profile? But Jeff Hancock doesn't believe*
*that the anonymity of the internet encourages dishon-*
*esty. In fact, he says the searchability and permanence*
*of information online may even keep us honest.*[28]

It's true.  Many employers, especially the small "Mom and Pop" businesses now look up a potential new employee through social media sites.  An employer can easily navigate a records search on a prospective employee to find everything from speeding tickets to bankruptcies.  Social media often finds postings that would be deemed inappropriate for an adult just by checking the name on Facebook.

Dating sites are rife with misinformation—so much so that many singles dismiss them as a harbinger for predators.  Photos posted are often decades old.  Generic hobbies are listed to cast a wide net in order to attract a willing partner who in unwillingly deceived.  But because these are semi-anonymous activities, the lies are rationalized as permissible for an ignoble purpose.

Cadet graduates are inured with the simple and easily re-citable honor code.  It becomes the guideline of lifetime ethics and morality.  It assists the graduate in his or her assessment of others in the workplace and in the social environment.  It follows that the expectations of those ethical standards will remain in force always.  The cadet honor code, then, is not a four-year contract with a college administration.  It is a life-long contract with self.

# *Self-Discipline*

Discipline seems like an imposition forced upon a student during a cadet career in a military environment.  But the graduate walks away with self-discipline as an asset.  We find that discipline is actually a self-imposed value that promotes planning, timing, and execution.  Though discipline in the cadet sense is restrictive—as it might relate to consequences rendered for the lack of discipline—the graduate value is an enhancement that lasts a lifetime.  Self-discipline becomes the foundation.

*"I did one hundred pounds.  Two hundred should be next, right?"*
*From the Mind of Ray Mayer.*

What have those four years wrought? Self-discipline should be near the top the list of virtues. It is because the entirety of a person's character is related to personal discipline.

The introduction to this book references The Citadel's *Blue Book*. As cadets can attest, the *Blue Book* becomes the code of discipline for the four-year system of behavior.

> *One commonly accepted dictionary definition of discipline has three parts. The first is 'control gained by enforcing obedience or order.' As part of The Citadel Experience, discipline in this context relates to a cadet's development as a leader. The second is 'orderly or prescribed conduct or pattern of behavior.' As part of The Citadel Experience, discipline in this context relates to the organizational culture and climate of The Citadel. The third is 'self-control.' As part of The Citadel Experience, discipline in this context relates to a cadet's development as an individual. Because discipline at The Citadel embraces all three of these contexts, the* Blue Book *is organized into chapters about organizational culture and climate, individual development, and leader development.* [29]

We can agree that the discipline carried forward refers to that of the third dictionary example—self-control. The discipline of self-control demands patience, planning, and vision. Great fortunes and rewarding lives have been built by Citadel graduates who adhered to the discipline of self-control.

Pat Conroy, the Southern literary giant from The Citadel Class of 1967, authored several books that became movies. He famously sequestered himself from the outside world while composing his chapters. He wrote on yellow pads with a goal to finish five pages each day.[30] He detailed that it was a matter of self-discipline to write an effective novel. His self-discipline to write productively, creatively, and effectively defined his high sense of art.

*The student activities center and The Citadel Gift Shop are housed in Mark Clark Hall.*
*One may find a number of literary offerings, including the works of Pat Conroy.*
*Photo by author.*

Conroy attributed much of his later-life success to The Citadel's rigid system that taught self-control. He furthered the learning experience in his novel *The Prince of Tides*.

> *Teach them the quiet verbs of kindness, to live be-*
> *yond themselves. Urge them toward excellence,*
> *drive them toward gentleness, pull them deep into*
> *yourself, pull them upward toward manhood, but*
> *softly like an angel arranging clouds.*[31]

It was no accident that the title of his third book, a 1980 bestseller that also became a movie, was *The Lords of Discipline*.

When Pat Conroy died in 2016, he had an arrangement with The Citadel Class of 2001 as its graduation speaker to flash their rings as exalted guests at his funeral. His funeral overflowed with attendees. His rigid upbringing in a military household and as a cadet at The Citadel, by his account, made for a lifetime of responsibility and a surge of emotions that served him well.

By another example, Dr. Harvey Schiller, The Citadel Class of 1960, has perhaps the finest résumé of any cadet graduate ever. Schiller served as U.S. Olympic Committee Executive Director and as chairman of *YankeeNets*—owner of the New York Yankees, New Jersey Nets, and New Jersey Devils. He served the country as an Air Force pilot in Vietnam (1,100 missions) and rose to the rank of brigadier general. Schiller's impressive career highlights include service as America's Cup Commissioner (international yacht racing), on the board of the Baseball Hall of Fame, and as president of the International Baseball Federation and Turner Broadcasting Sports.

Schiller held many other leadership roles to include that of Commissioner of the NCAA's Southeastern Conference. It was not a popular stance he took while applying for the SEC commissioner's role. A 2009 *New York Times* article noted the exchange.

> *The Citadel provided discipline, a regimented approach to life. Years later, while interviewing with the SEC, Schiller told the university presidents that he had come from an institution that did not lie, steal, cheat, or tolerate anyone who did. He said they represented institutions with all four vices.*[32]

The articulate and highly disciplined Schiller was hired. The college presidents recognized their reputational shortcomings and sought to reverse the pattern. Schiller was unafraid to effect change and likely would not have undertaken the position under any other circumstance.

Self-discipline, then, is a constant throughout life. It is the self-imposed barrier one expects of oneself.

> *Self-discipline is one of the most important and useful skills everyone should possess. This skill is essential in every area of life, and though most people acknowledge its importance, very few do something to strengthen it. Contrary to common belief, building self-discipline does not mean being harsh with yourself, or living a limited, restrictive lifestyle. Building this skill means using common sense, making priorities, and thinking before acting.*

*Self-discipline means self-control, which is a sign of inner strength and control of yourself and your reactions. This skill gives you the power to stick to your decisions and follow them through, without changing your mind. It is one of the important requirements for achieving your goals and carrying out tasks.*

*Studies show that students with a high degree of this skill retained more knowledge than those without it. This is because they are more persevering and possess the inner strength to focus on their studies.[33]*

It is discipline that connects to all other tenets of behavior. Wouldn't self-discipline top the list of virtues that we should teach our children? It makes all else much the easier.

The counterculture of the 1960s and 1970s brought America to "the ledge" in many ways. A rampant drug culture was a root cause. The sense of self-discipline had receded to the perimeter of society. It would take a full generation to bring it back to the center. As a result, senseless deaths were attributed to overdoses and excessive behaviors went unchecked. The discipline to say "No!" was the exception, not the rule. As a result, a sad list exists of celebrities who died before their 30th birthday from unfortunate lifestyle choices. Many led to harmful addictions and drug overdoses—Jimi Hendrix, Jim Morrison, Duane Allman, River Phoenix, Amy Winehouse, Heath Ledger, Kurt Cobain, Jean-Michel Basquiat, Janis Joplin, and too many others to name here.[34]

This lack of self-discipline persists in our culture as so many adults struggle with alcohol addictions and the more recent introduction of opioid medications. Much of the misery that could be spared to a family, loved ones, and especially the victim would have harbored no stead had self-discipline been strengthened in early life. It is the unruly and often destructive effect of lacking self-discipline that deteriorates a productive and honorable life.

# *Ingenuity*

Many moons have passed since the 1970s, when knobs like me found that being invisible was the goal of the plebe system. The unofficial Knob Creed: Do not draw attention to thyself! I broke that rule, once.

It was nearing Corps Day when our Oscar Company freshman class was gently persuaded to have a bedsheet sign at the ready for the Saturday morning in-barracks visits by alumni and parents. My friends and classmates in Oscar Company were having a particularly difficult time coming up with ideas the weekend prior—and we were not allowed general leave until we completed the project. I volunteered that we had eight members of the junior class vying to become Summerall Guards. We could name them on the sheet if we could incorporate them into the psychedelic lyrics of a newly popular song, "Spill the Wine". The song, performed by the band War, started with the lyrics, "I was once out strolling one very hot summer's day." That was an inviting lead-in. We simply corrupted the following paced lyrics to include the last names of our Bond Volunteer aspirants. Our song-contrived company bedsheet was a hit. The BVs loved it. Many of the upperclassmen were appreciative of the ingenuity our class presented to the public who would invade Oscar Company the following week.

The artistic bedsheet hung from the fourth division and drew smiles from everyone, it seemed. Things were looking up, and we were only six weeks from the "Old Corps"

Recognition Day that would occur toward the end of the academic year.

*Barracks are open at Homecoming and Corps Day each year.*
*Note the bedsheets from the fourth division.*
*Photo by author.*

After Corps Day weekend, a senior officer platoon leader stood in front of our formation as we were bracing for evening mess. He yelled out, "Which one of you idiots came up with the "Spill the Wine" idea?" No one answered immediately. The platoon leader repeated the question a bit louder, giving us the sense that we would all be punished. I answered. Whoops. I mistakenly thought there might be a chance that this irascible senior platoon leader would say something nice.

"McQueeney, you &%$@*#, I hate that song. Drive by my room after mess," the platoon leader barked.

I was wise enough not to eat much at that evening meal. While I cannot blame that event on ingenuity, I can blame it on breaking the rule of invisibility. Had I divulged that song idea as it actually was—a joint knob enterprise—I would not have been spared a sweaty evening of hazing. Instead, we would have had an event for which this senior was famous— a knob sweat party at the third division shower room at zero-four-thirty.

Fortunately, The Citadel does not tolerate illegal activity, and hazing has become an expulsion offense. I often thought that the hazing rule should have been applied 50 years retroactively. Hazing, at its essence, represents a lack of leadership...and ingenuity.

The ingenuity gained as a cadet was seen in both a positive and rules-breaking sense. We couldn't keep coffee makers or TV sets in the barracks. We definitely couldn't have liquor or firecrackers. That big word we knew from the *Blue Book* was "contraband." Yet these *Blue Book* cancellation items nevertheless existed within the Corps of Cadets through the devious ingenuity of those accepting risk.

There were cadet-legal ways to exhibit ingenuity in the barracks. A junior I knew from high school told me years later that he made a fortune copying 8-track tapes from LP albums in his room down in First Battalion. Because of the then-popularity of 8-track players and long drives home during furlough, his recording work was often found in high demand.

My rickety old aqua-cased typewriter was cadet-legal. I made a quarter per ERW ("Explanation of Report,

Written"—frequently referred to in cadet parlance as "Excuse Required in Writing"). My company sent in a lot of ERWs. There was also the legitimate opportunity to type out someone's hand-written term paper. The typing experts charged by the page (as I recall). Every company had at least one very busy and well-paid typist in the cadet steno pool.

And there were countless other cadet-legal pursuits with a marketing plan. There were cadets selling tee-shirts, filling in for weekend guard duty for a price, offering grilled cheese sandwiches at bargain prices in the battalion, or selling cadet furlough ride shares from the company bulletin board. Typically, the board would read, "Driving to Scranton, PA. Will take up to three passengers for $20 each."

Local rides around town were sold, too. It is not surprising that the ingenuity of the Corps of Cadets came up with the earliest form of Uber.

There were the adventurous drivers, too. Some cadets made "cannonball runs" to "Mickey D's" during Evening Study Period (ESP) for a price. It seems that there was more enterprise in marketing services being conducted outside of the *Blue Book* regulations. Another set of roommates bought a "Rock 'em Sock 'em Robot's" game. It turned out to be an enterprise. They set up tournaments, entry fees, and a betting function. It was the first unwitting analog version of the Xbox video game console tournaments that take place during ESP today.

A Class of 1972 Tango Company junior private and his roommate had the corner on Fourth Battalion grilled cheese and hotdogs market during ESP for two years running. These entrepreneurs claimed the non-existent concessionaire's license for the battalion. Back then, knobs would not have an option to "pass" on a warm food offering—at fifty cents apiece. We can call it unsanctioned, against the *Blue Book* regulations, or even opportunistic. We should also consider that it was an impressive form of creativity, ingenuity, and entrepreneurship that made the most a controlled and inviting market.

Hiding the portable rabbit-eared television or the coffeemaker took skill during an SMI (Saturday Morning Inspection). I do not remember anyone in my company having either item confiscated. Yet these items were clearly outlawed in our *Blue Books*.

If a mischief-plotting cadet could afford to execute a cherry bomb explosion in a trashcan at midnight just outside of a first sergeant's room, it could—and would—be arranged. This entire scenario would fall under the category of contraband items illegally utilized during restricted hours. But it happened often. Cadets loved to prank other cadets.

There were curious rule violations, too, that had no plan for profit. One cadet in my company kept an iguana for an entire semester. As a junior private, he pulled it off. I had never seen an iguana and mistakenly assumed that they were ferocious. They are docile herbivores. They didn't like the mess hall fare, either.

In a general sense, civilization has always been advanced by ingenuity. Cities were founded near fresh water, but their livability was not improved until ingenuity solved the issue of moving the water—by aqueducts, by water wheels, by pumps—and by moving the citizens over or across the water, and then by moving their waste away from the city. All advancements to culture have roots in singular or collective ingenuity. Civilized people find ways to overcome the elements, the animals, and their enemies.

Ingenuity comes in all sizes, shapes, and categories. Wartime ingenuity changed many wars. For instance, the *chevaux de frise* (variously *cheval de frise*) was a defensive mechanism. The French word "frise," meaning "curly," references the impressive Friesian horses used by the Spanish. The rival Dutch were seeking independence from Spain. Their defensive ingenuity was to place long spikes in multiple directions from central logs to halt the cavalry charge of the highly regarded Spanish cavalry. The Dutch eventually gained their independence from Spain in 1648,[35] aided by the ingenuity of this countermeasure against the impressive Friesian horse cavalry. Wartime advancements, unfortunately, fill a large segment of "historical ingenuity."

Ingenuity is a learned commodity that is fertilized when others are called in to participate. The Corps of Cadets became acclimated to the culture of joint imagination and adventure.

If "necessity is the mother of invention," then ingenuity is its mentoring uncle. We can marvel at how time advances an idea. Orville Wright was the first to successfully master flight in Kitty Hawk, North Carolina. The year was 1903.[36] Wright's flight velocity was estimated at 30 miles per hour. By rapidly expanding the concept of flight, a velocity greater than the speed of sound (the sound barrier) was breached before Orville Wright died in 1948.[37] The pilot was Chuck Yeager, who recorded the feat in October of 1947, forty-four years removed from the first manned flight.[38] A mere fourteen years later, in 1961, astronaut Alan Shepherd piloted the first U.S.-manned spaceflight.[39]  Mankind can take the basic idea and magnify the impact by ingenious means.

Ingenuity is a pillar of commerce, invention, science, and even survival.  The element of ingenuity is admired in every facet of humanity and has become part of the culture of the Corps of Cadets.  In this close-knit, challenging environment, the group effort to solve and succeed has thrived.  The culture remains that there is more to know than is known.

Since 2011, the STEM Center at The Citadel has hosted the annual "Storm The Citadel!"[40] event, inviting the community and local students to marvel at a working trebuchet competition.  The event included other engineering feats in robotics and even water bottle rockets.  Cadets took the active mentoring role.  The earliest trebuchets and catapults date back to the fifth century.[41]  Enterprising cadets made them come alive again for Lowcountry primary and secondary school students.

The expansion of the creative mind is perhaps an underlying enchantment of college curricula.  It is found both inside and beyond the classroom.

*Creativity has many definitions, and it can mean different things to everyone, depending upon one's perspective. One definition of creative is having the ability to turn new imaginative ideas into reality. When this natural love of curiosity doesn't have a place to thrive, we all lose when it comes to potential talent and entrepreneurship.[42]*

Beyond-the-diploma entrepreneurship arose from the cross-communication of cadet-generated resourcefulness. Given space and imagination, cadets learn the lifelong values of resourcefulness from those before them. Imagination thrives... and sometimes this characteristic is seen in the artistic Corps Day bedsheets created by knobs that adorn the fourth division rails of each cadet company.

# A Time for Respect

During the COVID-19 ordeal felt worldwide, several public outcries emerged. The pandemic deterrence community of immunopathologists highly recommended the wearing of facemasks. At times, the containment effectiveness of facemasks was brought into question. Across the nation, people verbally assaulted others who chose not to wear the mask in public as an infringement upon their constitutional rights. The world had turned upside down.

Other deep social issues arose. These were not limited to The Citadel, to a region, or to the social fabric of the United States. The world was reeling and trying to readjust societal interactions by a single measure of value—human respect—became omnipresent.

The sense of respect among fellow human beings had dissipated. There were greater concerns beyond a pandemic. Yet within the pandemic, other divisions surfaced.

Whether or not one believed in the efficacy of facemasks, there seemed to be little concern about respecting others who may have had heightened medical risk reasons to warrant every precaution. It was for their benefit that the right to wear or not to wear facemasks should have been pre-empted. It was a matter of respect.

*The Thomas Dry Howie Bell Tower honors*
*a Citadel WWII war hero.*
*Photo by author.*

Even after effective vaccines were dispensed, the newly vaccinated still wore facemasks. Why? To allay the fears of those who had not been vaccinated. This, too, was a matter of societal respect for the plight of others.

The virtuous extension of respect to all factions has become much more public than in times past. There are areas of life where interpersonal relationships find their foundation in respect. The age-old interaction of gender-respect seems to evolve with modern nuances. At The Citadel, this became a transition in earnest as females first attended the institution in the late 1990s. The rapid adjustment took place not only with respect to regulations and bathrooms, but to the interactions required among a cadet chain of command within a closed system mired in traditions. Change was imminent.

The most far-reaching change that had to occur was the advance of equality relationships within an organized and disciplined environment. This evolution gave rise to the key element of inter-gender respect in every facet of cadet life and discourse. As a result, the immersion of female cadets into the Corps of Cadets had to depend upon careful judgment and equitable order that enhanced cadet character in the form of respect. The *Blue Book* expanded. Some issues took time to adapt—female haircuts, physical fitness standards, privacy, and athletic competition. Other issues became naturally adjustable to the system, such as academic achievement, leadership opportunities, and chain-of-command practices.

Without the cross-respect for others, society becomes subject to predatory influences. The news, too often, reports the carnage. We see the landmark cases from Hollywood producers and actors to Wall Street tycoons. It appears that success often brings with it a sense of invincibility. People begin to believe that they are above the restrictions of law and the trust engendered within societal interactions. Affluence buys influence and influence too often digresses to the confluence of narcissism and ill intent. The sad fall can be seen on the magazine racks of every grocery line.

Respect reaches deeply into cultural and racial interactions as well. The respect for others' points of view and ideology became significant and fostered heathy interchanges among cadets. It became important that no cadet becomes ostracized from others because of any perceived difference—gender, religion, race, sexual orientation, economic standing, or ideology. A cadet must adapt to the higher attainment of respect for all others, despite differences.

There is not any specific reason that the lack of respect for others emerges in society. There could be pre-perceived notions, diverse social environments, or even odd religious inhibitions. Often, the lack of respect and the prospect of unacceptable positions of inequality can be remaindered to economic overtones.

> *Contemporary concerns over inequality are typically framed in economic terms. Income and wealth provide convenient gauges of the growing distance between the affluent and the rest. But there is a much deeper kind of inequality, caused not by a lack of resources, but by a lack of respect. You might be much richer or poorer than I am. But if we treat each other with mutual respect, we are, relationally speaking, equal. Societies that are equal in terms of relations are those in which there is mutual respect, where – as the philosopher Philip Pettit put it in 2010, alluding to a line by John Milton – 'free persons … can speak their minds, walk tall among their fellows, and look each other squarely in the eye'.*[43]

"Equality" in every sense of the word heightened the ideal of respect. In so many ways over so many years, the goal of equal opportunity and equality of standing had been breached. At The Citadel, equality found a system of codified, required, and enforced guidelines that create a level playing field by stripping incoming cadets of their privileges to enhance the ideals of respect for a lifetime. The *Blue Book* is blind to all influences. Breaking those tenets—those *Blue Book* rules—had and has consequences. Any detour from proper decorum and due respect for all can easily denigrate into disrespect and is not tolerated. Lack of respect is a breach of decency to all of society.

The world has slowly adjusted to the higher plateau of respect for all peoples. Yet cadet graduates have already shown the highest aptitude for this quality. Respect for others is a conscious choice that serves the person and the whole of society well.

# *Acceptance of Leadership*

Mayors and mentors—chairmen, principals, and council-women—all share roots in The Citadel's proven system of preparing graduates for leadership roles. When called upon, graduates are armed with the knowledge and insight required of them to lead. In so many selfless ways, graduates are prepared for the moment to step forward. Those tools of time management, organization, and charitable intent mesh to provide communities, small and large, with able and deeply committed leaders.

A publication extolling the *Ten Virtues of Outstanding Leadership*[44] by Al Gini and Ronald Green indicates exemplary historical models. The authors cite deep honesty, moral courage, moral vision, compassion and care, fairness, intellectual excellence, creative thinking, aesthetic sensitivity, good timing, and deep selflessness.

These tenets of selfless and virtuous leadership are excellent insights. The Citadel's wide and focused experience also fosters other critical elements—capacity, adaptability, overcoming obstacles, communication, time management, and team building.

Another general view from the Northeastern Masters in Leadership program describes the width of leadership aptly by portraying five qualities commonly found in leaders.

1. *They are self-aware and prioritize personal development.*

2. *They focus on developing others.*

3. *They encourage strategic thinking, innovation, and action.*

4. *They are ethical and civic-minded.*

5. *They practice effective cross-cultural communication.*[45]

Leadership within a community entails wider values because, often, that leadership role may enlist unpaid volunteers to a cause. It may be a school fundraiser or a benefit for a hospital. In these charitable endeavors, it may be asserted that effective leadership will require much more personality and patience. This is a different kind of leadership and almost always requires that those leaders employ the consequence of giving of self. Charitable community leadership, then, would add other group-friendly and exemplary elements.

In the military, leadership is designated. However, regardless of one's rank or position, there are often many situational occasions to lead—those who present themselves in battle without the benefit of chain-of-command. The 3,500-plus Medal of Honor recipients bear this notion out—on the fields of conflict, in the air, and on the open sea. A compelling number of the Medal of Honor recipients—nearly half—earned their citation from within the ranks as non-commissioned officers.[46] When selflessness and leadership bravado were confronted by a high risk of death, the mettle of the person stood out.

Our society suffers from a dearth of principled leaders in our times. That condition can be seen across industry, politics, entertainment, and community. The news reports a seemingly unending stream of corruption, financial misdeeds, drug addictions, and violence related to those once held in high esteem. History is a darkened host. We have seen the Enron implosion, the financial schemes of Bernie Madoff, the 2008 financial crisis, college admission corruption, church leadership scandals, and the nearly constant political corruption exposés. It seems that corporate power and celebrity, too often, end with shootings, overdoses, and suicides. And that's just in the United States. The world, at large, is much worse. One only needs to research the words "political scandal" or "financial corruption" to find deeper and more troubling reports coming from Germany, Venezuela, South Africa, and Turkey, among countless other countries. The sense of human decency is at risk.

Society could become complicit. When there are times to display decency, that act alone represents leadership. An excerpt extolling leadership by demanding decency makes the point clear.

*...there are times when you won't feel comfortable making a public display of disapproval. In these situations, the very least that you can do is to show support for the person who has been at the brunt of rude or mean behavior...our basic human instinct is to protect each other and to be empathetic, we invariably see moments in our daily lives when feelings are hurt, either intentionally or not. In those moments a kind gesture or word can make a difference in someone's day. We must for our*

*community—and really for all of humanity—do*
*our very best to help others have the confidence to*
*lead productive and fulfilling lives.*[47]

Leading is often the act of bravery to convince others the internal concept of accepting their own leadership by self-respect, dignity, and truth.

The Citadel continues to lead by example. The administration emplaced an academic course of study on leadership and even offers a minor degree in leadership for those cadets inclined to participate. The program is offered directly under the auspices of the college's provost and has a carefully planned curriculum that teaches conditional and situational leadership practices.

*Congresswoman Nancy Mace, Class of 2000, became the first female*
*graduate of The Citadel.*
*She was elected as the First Congressional District of South Carolina*
*representative in 2020.*
*Photo provided by The Citadel.*

Leadership matters. Leadership, with honor, may be the most focused precept of character imparted to each Citadel graduate. These are the indispensable lifelong tools that build families, strengthen relationships, and shape societies.

We must always ask ourselves how we can make the world around us a better place? Can we mentor or teach? Can we volunteer or serve? In all things we must internalize leading ourselves in an honorable manner first, and then we can lead others.

# *Spirituality*

More and more, the sense of spirituality has been remanded to the individual. The Citadel has regular religious services that are optional to the Corps of Cadets—much as church and synagogue attendance is optional to the cadet graduates. Traditional church memberships have been on a decline across both the United States and the world at large.

Only half of the United States population affiliates with a church. A few decades ago, that number was 70 percent.[48]

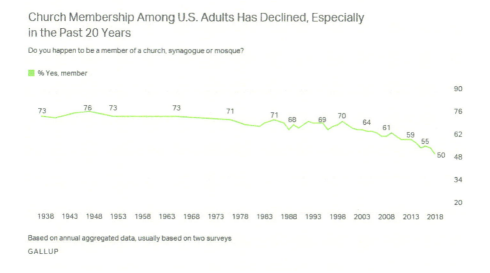

Church Membership Among U.S. Adults Has Declined, Especially in the Past 20 Years

Do you happen to be a member of a church, synagogue or mosque?

% Yes, member

Based on annual aggregated data, usually based on two surveys
GALLUP

*The decline of church affiliation and attendance trends downward. Gallup research chart.*

Cadets may opt for services of their spiritual persuasion or refrain entirely. The requirement to attend services that once was in place became passé in 1972 with a Supreme Court decision. Yet cadets especially found attendance to be beneficial to their life goals.

Though it is normal to separate church attendance from spirituality, the existence of the latter has prominence in cadet life and beyond. One pundit noted that spirituality grew exponentially as the Corps of Cadets moved closer to final exams. We may surmise that spirituality grows to vault one past the skeptics, the atheists, and the agnostics as the aging process brings one to the last of life's final exams.

Albert Einstein was widely known to be an agnostic and often took other views. He wrote in a letter to a friend in 1954, "If God created the world, his primary concern was certainly not to make its understanding easy for us."[49] He had also advanced the sense of Godly order in his lectures by repeating that there had to be a "prime mover."

Here's another interpretation of that reasoning: What exactly would the unfaithful have to lose as even a casual believer? If one has no belief in a life beyond, okay. But just suppose that view turns out to be wrong. What was given up for the convenience of living out the life of a skeptic? One might argue several beneficial answers that would impact the life of a person immersed in faith. There's the giant word itself—faith. There is faith among believers for the salvation of the soul. Faith is what compels those reinforced in their discipline of faith to pray, to expand their knowledge of faith, and to lead others in faith. Faith is what often binds a community or even a nation. And in faith we often find the goodness expected in people—for love of mankind, for timely and selfless charity, and for healing—physically, emotionally, and mentally.

The secular world has a place that can be said is best supported by the benefits of religion. Why? The secular world adheres to law. The religious world goes much farther. It relies on conscience. There is a sense of what is morally right or wrong, regardless of what the law states.

> *Religion is a fundamental part of human dignity. For many adherents, it is far more than a mere lifestyle choice, it is the deepest part of who they are. To violate a person's religious freedom or require them to act against their religious beliefs or practices violates the very core of that person's being. Sociological studies have shown positive benefits of religious affiliation for school performance, positive family life, well-being and contribution to community life. Religions also provide for rites of passage such as marking birth, marriage and death.[50]*

In a world in which religion has especially been sidelined by a pandemic, in addition to the after-effects of apathy and many internal scandals, holding spirituality with adherence to sacred scripture has increasingly become anathema. Prevailing governmental intrusions seem to fall well aside of organized religion. So much of religion has become internal to the individual. It has been strengthened by a resurgence of Bible study groups and several evangelical megachurches. Cadet graduates have a potpourri from which to choose—or not choose. However, the cadet trend mirrors the lessons of good citizenship. Cadets are much more likely to be spiritually motivated and involved in formal religion than the general population. They find solace in their respective avenues of faith.

Nationally, trends have developed. The megachurches surge. Churches like Saddleback Valley Community (California), Lakewood Church (Houston), and Seacoast Church (Mount Pleasant, SC) boast congregations over 10,000. Some reach 40,000 weekly attendees. Religion is alive...it's just found in different places and poses different motivations.

However, the traditional religions continue to lose their congregations. It appears to be a generational concern.

> *As is the case with religious affiliation, generational replacement also is helping to drive lower levels of religious commitment. In other words, **as older, more religiously observant generations die out, they are being replaced by far less religious young adults**. One example: Two-thirds of members of the Silent generation (67%) say religion is very important in their lives, but only 38% of the youngest members of the Millennial generation – those born between 1990 and 1996 – say the same. Just 28% of these youngest Millennials report attending religious services at least weekly, compared with about half (51%) of their Silent generation counterparts.* [51]

There has not been a study conducted to assess what religious affiliations and attendance have meant within the Corps of Cadets or to life after The Citadel. The access to religion has been prevalent and its participation has been advocated. Perhaps a better assessment could be to quantify those graduates who assume religious leadership roles within their lives as a priority—ministers, pastors, priests, deacons, and rabbis.

Whether or not religion plays a major guidance role in the lives of graduates is conjecture. There have been no surveys to extrapolate the data. Yet, the campus environment seems to reflect a highly positive regard for a significant majority of cadets who uphold the value of faith in their personal lives.

Parenthetically, sustaining a deep-rooted spirituality beyond religious affiliation has another place to enumerate success. Religion has—for the entirety of The Citadel's existence—been a highly visible and widely available avenue in the lives of cadets.

*A view of Padgett Thomas Barracks from Jenkins Hall.*
*Photo by author.*

# Section Three: Engagement

As time marches the years in rows behind us, it makes sense to solidify all the elements of the life being led. There are spouses and children. There are careers and incursions into the delightful other areas of life—friendships, avocations, and community endeavors. We find that the joy of life becomes commensurate with the joy placed into life's effort. We engage.

When our *Blue Book of Life* is considered, can we reflect upon the things we found were the hardened rules never to be broken? Can we reflect in earnest the times when we gave back—even if those gifts were minimal but above what we might have been able to afford at the time? Have we used our experiences in a mentoring light to help others? Have we changed the lives of others in a positive fashion? What is our PHC (Positive Human Consequence)?

Where we start often reflects back to where we got our start.

# Reunions & Other Gatherings

Graduates do not always come back for reunions. There are numerous obstacles. Some in the military are stationed in faraway places. Some in careers cannot take the time. Some have economic considerations. Some have familial responsibilities that supersede reunions. And there are some that just do not want to come. So be it.

There are exceptions to nearly every maxim. As a rule, Citadel graduates come back. They lived a unique period of their lives in a closed society. They like the other side of life beyond and come back to share their stories, their insights, and their blessings. The major event that attracts graduates is the Homecoming weekend of the fall football schedule. That weekend boasts a full agenda for returning "ring-knockers." These include an open barracks invitation and mess hall visit, a likely Summerall Guard performance, and a full-dress cadet Homecoming parade. Of course, there will be a football game and various organized alumni parties—most notably the StrayDog Jamboree.

Though the larger gatherings are for the classes that return in multiples of five-year anniversaries, all graduates may participate.

Another major gathering is Corps Day weekend, hosted each spring on a weekend adjacent to March 20, the anniversary celebrating the day the first class of cadets reported to Marion Square in 1843. It is during Corps Day that the college salutes those graduates who have returned to solidify relationships initiated in the barracks life of a military college student. These relationships form a strong bond.

The college offers other ample opportunities. There are the many sports that are not college football. Attendance at a spring baseball game at Joseph P. Riley, Jr., Park is one of the elevated experiences of the Charleston outdoors. The park is among the best minor league parks in America and is named for the beloved forty-year mayor of Charleston, who graduated with the Class of 1964.

There are so many annualized events emanating from the schools of discipline—Engineering, Education, Business, Science and Mathematics, and Humanities and Social Sciences. Each has gained a unique personality.

The Citadel Foundation (TCF) also adds workshop events into the schedule. They bring in outstanding speakers and advocate the cross-pollination of class representatives who share entrepreneurial ideas, alumni stories, and plenty of reminiscence.

Years ago, I was asked to speak at the Corps Day festivities of the Great Northwest Citadel Club. The evening program in Seattle, Washington, was well-attended with graduates young and older. I was pleasantly surprised at the healthy interchanges and the annual muster—the traditional roll call of those who had passed in the prior year. These alumni meetings take place all over the country. They are well-structured and advocated by The Citadel Alumni Association, and they are a powerful way for the community of Citadel brothers and sisters to gather together in memory of those we have lost.

The Citadel is here, there, and everywhere. It is up to the graduates to avail themselves of the opportunities.

# Military Service

At various times, the Military College of South Carolina has supplied an abundance of skilled personnel across the four major military services. There is even an active U.S. Coast Guard ROTC (Reserve Officer Training Corps) detachment. Every cadet participates in ROTC and receives military training—inside and outside of the classroom. Every cadet is expected to be physically fit—in a parallel standard that emulates military service fitness. Yet the graduate experience of serving in the military is not a requirement of the college. Because it is an option, more cadets are able to gain a sense of the commitment through their first two years of cadet life before deciding upon a career military contract, if offered. This option likewise allows The Citadel to become more adaptable to the various non-military career plans of the Corps of Cadets.

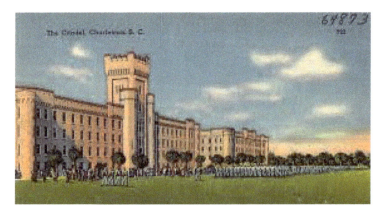

*The Marion Square facility housed the*
*military college from 1842 to 1922.*

There is certainly an inside-the-military connection between Citadel graduates. These connections transcend class years, with the emphasis upon a similar cadet experience. In so many ways, cadet companies have their own identities but meld together over the years into the significant commonality shared among those who wear the ring.

Citadel graduates serving in the military form a unique bond. One may see pictured in the college's *Alumni News* magazine a group of cadets in the military from several classes at a faraway base assignment, their rings pointing outward toward the camera and the world. Graduates often assemble at military bases across the service to celebrate their heritage of cadet life years prior.

It has also become a recognizable trend that an alumnus vying for one of the three Citadel Alumni Association seats on the college's trustee board, The Citadel Board of Visitors, will likely espouse a military service background. Thus, the military service of cadet graduates is fully represented in the board room where decisions are made to impact the future of The Citadel.

The college produces principled leaders. That benefit is never more apparent than in the process of graduating young men and women into the service of the nation.

*The Citadel War Memorial lists those who have made*
*the ultimate sacrifice*
*dating from the Mexican War of 1848 to the present day.*
*The memorial encompasses the grave of General Mark Clark*
*and the Thomas Dry Howie Carillon.*
*Nearly 500 graduates have died in wartime conflict.*

In terms of military engagement, The Citadel remains well outside of societal norms. We send many to serve. These are our most honored graduates who have pledged to defend our nation come what may. There are nearly five hundred

Citadel graduates who have rendered the ultimate salute to our flag with their lives. All are appropriately commended at the center of The Citadel's campus with a solemn Citadel War Memorial. It is a place of peace and reflection.

As a result of decreasing call for military officers nationwide, The Citadel's output to the five services has dwindled over the years, and many graduates who experienced the college's military training benefit often follow other civilian callings. The decrease in military participation is not remaindered to The Citadel alone. Society has, in effect, placed military service in the attic. Serving the country is an afterthought – a vestige of times past – that at times has international consequences. A strong military from a country bordered by two large oceans no longer engenders a sense of isolation and deterrence. We must be ready always.

Putting the ratio of military service in perspective across the entirety of America's population reveals stunning statistics. Justin Naylor, a farmer from Northeastern Pennsylvania, underscores the facts.

> *Like many Americans today, I don't know many veterans, either living or deceased. And like many Americans today, not only did I not serve in the military, but I never even considered it while I was growing up. Among my fellow Americans, I'm not alone or unusual. While about 9% of the population fought in WWII, today's active-duty military comprises about 0.5% of the population—a little more than one million people, down from two million just before the end of the Cold War.*

*To put it bluntly, we have outsourced the common defense to a tiny minority of our fellow Americans, and military service is no longer a defining characteristic of the American experience. For most Americans, waging war no longer takes a personal toll nor demands personal sacrifice. Our wars are fought, not by our friends, and family, and neighbors, but by "other people" with whom we rarely or never interact. I don't have a single friend or family member who fought in Iraq or Afghanistan. This separation from the reality and costs of war has serious consequences, I think, both for our culture at large, and for each of us personally.[52]*

It is those "other people" who serve. In so many cases, those people are classmates, sons or daughters, and friends we lost touch with as they moved from base to base protecting our country and our democracy. A military veteran is a national treasure.

The proud military tradition continues at The Citadel. The military component enmeshed with higher education became the 1842 founding purpose. That 99.5% of our country who enjoy the benefit of those willing to lay down their lives is too often detached from the reality. We should salute all who serve and have served daily. A simple "Thank you for your service" goes a long way to that purpose.

*The Seraph Monument was donated by the British Parliament to honor Citadel president, General Mark Wayne Clark (1954-1965). This British submarine delivered General Clark to Algeria in 1942 on a covert mission to inform the French of an impending Allied landing.*

# *Looking Back by Looking Forward*

From time to time, I have been called upon to speak to a targeted audience. A few years ago (2012), I had the privilege of speaking to the Daniel Fund Scholars at The Citadel. It gave me a chance to reflect upon what The Citadel educational experience meant to me over a lifetime. I kept a calm focus upon a reverent topic that I believed encompassed the feelings of most graduates. I explained to the cadet and faculty audience that I had arrived at The Citadel from unusual circumstances. My heartfelt address is reprinted below from its original form.

> *Good afternoon. The meal was free, and they're not paying the speaker. So, you're in for a cheap thrill.*
>
> *My being here in front of you requires a perspective.*
>
> *I grew up in a family with eight siblings. Our four-room rental home was old, dank, and chaotic. I learned how to box at the age of five just to be able to get into the only bathroom. Six boys slept in the same bedroom. Despite the circumstances, we were rich in every notion—with the obvious exception of money. My World War II U.S. Navy veteran father had been poorer than we were. He grew up admiring The Citadel. He directed each of us selflessly*

*by the vestige of his hollowed dreams. "You're all going to college, and that's not up for discussion," he commanded. And all nine of us went to college. By his determination, six sons graduated from The Citadel.*

*When my oldest brother, Danny, finished high school, my father gave him a choice. He could go anywhere he desired as long as the college he chose was on the banks of the Ashley River.*

*I arrived on the campus of The Citadel in August of 1970. My perspective was simple. The Citadel was my first experience where I knew—with certainty—that I was going to get three meals a day. I received new clothes, too! There were no more hand-me-downs! There were free haircuts. I only had one roommate. And to me, that barracks room was enormous. Air conditioning? That was for sissies.*

*We had some different rules back then, but nothing that I couldn't handle or mishandle. All formations—three a day—were mandatory. I mostly liked the military formations. It meant that we were going to march, to run, or to eat. I had no issue with any of those choices. I was not the most polished cadet, but I notice today that I always have the best-shined shoes on any airplane. That should count for something!*

*There was also mandatory chapel attendance on Sunday. Heck, I had that situation since I was a toddler. It made for a lifetime habit I still enjoy. And after chapel, the best meal of the week was available—Sunday Brunch at the Mess Hall. Where else could one find grits, french fries, scrambled eggs, fried chicken, and a banana? It was fantastic!*

*When I was a young student, the only air conditioning available to cadets was in the library. We thought that circumstance to be a conspiracy started by General Mark W. Clark so that the Corps of Cadets would know where the library was located on campus and would visit it often. We did. I got in some of my best naps as a knob up on the second floor. Even the librarians knew when I needed more shut eye.*

*In Charleston, my brogue has a name. They call it "Geechee." All the best politicians have it, like Fritz Hollings and Joe Riley. As an English major, it took twenty-one professors the full four years to eradicate the awkward tones and mispronunciations from my vocabulary. They worked diligently to get me through into polite and well-enunciated society. When I received my diploma on stage, I said to the college President, General Duckett, "Hay ya go, out-da-doe." I still have some leftover Geechee to use later.*

*The Citadel presented meaningful lifetime com-
monalities that the modern cadets share with the
"Old Corps"— seven that I wrote down and I'd like
to mention. You will not need to list them, because
when you leave this place, they will enlist you.*

1. *There is a word here that supersedes friendship.
   It's bigger than that. The word is "Classmate."
   Classmates will be there for you forever. Count
   on it. The only father who sent six sons to The
   Citadel died in March of 2011. Within seventy-
   two hours of that notice, I received seventy-five
   emails of condolence, insight, and inspiration
   from classmates. Seventy-five classmates stopped
   their lives long enough to care about mine. A
   classmate has the same number you have on
   their ring. That, in my opinion, becomes the
   strongest brotherhood-sisterhood association in
   all of America. You will never forget that you
   knobbed together and crossed that stage together.*

2. *Another commonality is a subtle moment that
   changes everything. We've all had that moment.
   It almost always happens in August when it's
   somewhere near 96 degrees. We'd be pestered
   by no-see-ums. We'd lack sleep and food. Our
   physical tiredness tested our mettle. We were
   bracing, eyes straight ahead, and three or more
   angry people would be yelling at us as if you
   were the dumbest person that ever lived. Then*

*there was that little voice that asked: "What in the world am I doing here?" It was then—at that precise moment—that we had to beat the urge of quitting back to its place well short of our perseverance. It's the resolve of that singular moment that remains. That moment carries you through a lifetime of adversity. Citadel people just don't quit!*

3. *The Citadel embraces an honor system that lurches forward in every facet of life—and each cadet will appreciate its impact always. "A cadet does not lie, cheat, or steal, nor tolerate those who do." You're a cadet always. Life has that same honor code. It commands your choices and standing within your profession. It rings true across society.*

4. *A warped sense of humor is the shield we carry to thwart a sense of pending adversity and ever-present urgency. It allows us to brave much and to laugh at the temporary falsehoods of life. It beats back fear. It conquers the impossible. Yes, cadets laugh at 'Dear John' letters. It's our institutional humor that nobody else understands. It's a knowing bond that brings on a brimming smile.*

5. *There is a sense that arises from our cadet experiences that thrusts us forward when the need*

*for leadership is the challenge. From corpora-
tions to families, boardrooms to rooms of the
bored, leadership fills a place where voids once
existed. Someone like you will lead at a critical
moment. Will you be the right leader leading
into the right direction? Good and selfless leaders are scarce. The Citadel teaches us leadership
from that first knob haircut until the diploma is
handed into our waiting white gloves.*

6. *The Citadel teaches time management. There
is no such thing as 9 to 5 as a cadet. There is
only pace and capacity. Capacity is always what
it takes to get the job done. Clocks only mark the
accomplishment.*

7. *Lastly, The Citadel Ring is simply a symbol, but
it is made of infinite value. It increases every
time a Citadel alumnus does something mag-
nificent. From astronaut Randy Bresnik (Class
of 1989) to former U.S. Olympic Executive
Director Harvey Schiller (Class of 1960), there
is a value remitted nearly constantly. The ring
has value well beyond its gold. Each graduate
will become a part of it. And each entrepreneur,
missionary, commanding officer, and celebrated
author will raise the value of my ring. Every
cadet in this room will add value to the ring I
wear proudly.*

*As part of The Citadel experience, cadets make it a long-term goal to help someone else in life. Those of you who will report down to my end of life, looking back at more than four decades like it was yesterday, should heed these words:*

**Dare to dream, dare to reach, dare to care, and care to give back!**

*It is stepping out of the smallness of one life to the largeness of meaning within a lifetime. When one looks back, it will be clear—**the lessons learned, the friendships earned, and the values discerned** grew exponentially from The Citadel experience. You will be welcomed into the eminent membership of those who wear the sign of the rare— The Citadel Ring."*

*I was honored to have the opportunity to review what the college meant to me and why I felt it to be important to give back. Too often we are so busy making a life that we forget to live it. Live a Citadel life, and you will live well.*

*Thank You."*

***Being near the marsh along the Ashley River has its challenges.***
***From the Mind of Ray Mayer.***

While my Daniel Fund Scholar luncheon speech was well received, I focused upon giving back in a very narrow sense—support of the college. I failed to broaden the topic—and it's lucky for the cadets that I kept it narrow. Many had one o'clock academic classes to attend. Yet, the average Citadel graduate gives back much, much more than their support of The Citadel. They step into life and find roles that are meaningful to their place of worship, their community, and their nation. The large contingent of military officers we have supplied contributed their wellbeing—none more than Marine Corps 2nd Lt. Shane Childers, '01, with the ultimate sacrifice.

Childers had been a MECEP student (Marine Enlisted Commissioning Education Program). Sadly, he became the first American military fatality of Operation Iraqi Freedom.

*Author Tommy McQueeney entered The Citadel Class of 1974.*
*Shown with brothers Danny (Class of 1971) and*
*Charlie (Class of 1972).*
*They were photographed in front of the Daniel Library in 1970.*

Civilian graduates rise to prominent roles within their field of expertise and ostensibly give back of their knowledge, time, and financial support to organizations that they admire. It is an inherent virtue. It would not be a stretch to suggest that Citadel graduates give more back per capita in ratio to their fortunes than nearly every graduate of every college. Statistics are not available, but I believe that they would bear this out because of the culture shared by graduates—a culture that they learned as students.

I was once asked by a successful high school friend, an attorney who was campaigning for the office of South Carolina Attorney General, to assist him to locate centers-of-influence in so many of South Carolina's small towns. I took the time to write out a few recommendations of Citadel graduates I knew in the small communities he planned to visit. After winning the statewide seat in the general election, my friend, the new South Carolina Attorney General (and a graduate of Notre Dame), commented to me, "I found out something about rural South Carolina. Every small town has a large influencer. And in nearly every case that person was a Citadel graduate."

## *The Lifelong Influence*

A smile arises. It may be from a flight attendant who recognized the ring or from the person pumping gas near you who saw the alumni sticker. Though there are only 39,000 living graduates (to include "CGC – The Citadel Graduate College), the brand has been well established. Everyone, it seems, has a "branding" story.

Interviewing for job opportunities after graduation may have been where the Citadel diploma first made a difference. There are amazing colleges all across America—many with academic pedigrees that elevate high interest in an applicant. What separates The Citadel?

An employer may be looking for much more than an achievement record focused upon an academic field of discipline. Perhaps time management matters… or an adherence to duty. Perhaps the company has had bad results in its past from employees lacking honor. The Citadel aura shines. Because of the wide access of information, employers know what it takes to become a Citadel graduate. They can appreciate an academic engagement that is much more comprehensive and demanding of the individual. The four-year experience will advance a competent candidate most favorably.

Inherent in The Citadel's growing reputational identification is the responsibility of graduates to foster the ideals of the college in their everyday associations. The wealth of character established over four years cannot dissipate over the next forty.

There is an expectation that must be lived within the graduate family going forward.

It is important that the influence travels well beyond job interviews and burgeoning careers. There are myriad situations in which the diploma becomes the parchment certification of what's inside the graduate. Careers command less than a third of a person's life experience. The mission of The Citadel is timeless.

*As a higher education institution, The Citadel's mission is to educate and develop our students to become principled leaders in all walks of life by instilling the core values of The Citadel in a disciplined and intellectually challenging environment. A unique feature of this environment for the South Carolina Corps of Cadets is the sense of camaraderie produced through teamwork and service to others while following a military lifestyle. The Citadel strives to produce graduates who have insight into issues, ideas, and values that are of importance to society. It is equally important that Citadel graduates are capable of both critical and creative thinking, have effective communication skills, can apply abstract concepts to concrete situations, and possess the methodological skills needed to gather and analyze information.*[53]

In time, a graduate will be called upon to organize an initiative, change an attitude, or command an audience for a cause. There will be community thrusts and church affairs.

There will be coaching experiences and even political activities to render the tenets of character learned on campus. Duty beckons. Will you be called upon to care for your parents in their twilight years, or perhaps to care for someone with special needs? Will you stand up when called upon to serve your community or even your country? Will you prove yourself a patriot? That ring indicates you will do these things because you find them to be part of who you have become—indeed, to define the consistency of who you are.

*Arland D. Williams, '57.*
*Photo courtesy The Citadel.*

The ring defined the life of Arland D. Williams, the Class of 1957 federal reserve bank examiner who was on Air Florida Flight 90 approaching Washington, D.C. Severe weather caused the flight to crash into the Potomac on January 3, 1982. Williams survived the crash and continued to command the situation by passing the helicopter rope to others as he marshalled the rescue. He continued the ultimate selflessness of catching and passing the rope. Eventually, before the helicopter could return for him, Williams went down with the sinking airplane and drowned. He saved the lives of others while foregoing his own rescue.

When former president Ronald Reagan served as the keynote speaker at The Citadel graduation in May of 1993, he could have spoken about the college's tremendous contributions to the armed forces, to industry, or to finance, medicine, or law. Instead, he retold the story of Arland D. Williams—a graduate twenty-five years removed who had given up his life in a dire situation so that others might live.

These are not singular events. It was a Citadel graduate, Major Charlie Hodges, '00, of the 320 Special Tactics Squadron, who took command of the rescue of a soccer team in submerged Thailand caves. The 2018 rescue had the world's attention. The intense operation's success was considered nearly miraculous. Major Hodges's father, Reverend Richard Hodges, '72, served as my Oscar Company first sergeant.

The famed General Charles Pelot Summerall served The Citadel for twenty-two years as president. In that role he decided to forego a salary—accepting one dollar per year as remuneration for the privilege of mentoring his Corps. He even composed a sense of cadet and graduate decorum known as The Citadel Code. His guidelines apply in every age for every person who has made The Citadel part of their educational experience.

**THE CITADEL CODE**

To revere God, love my country, and be loyal to The Citadel.

To be faithful, honest, and sincere in every act and purpose and to know that honorable failure is better than success by unfairness or cheating.

To perform every duty with fidelity and conscientiousness and to make duty my watchword.

To obey all orders and regulations of The Citadel and of proper authority.

To refrain from intoxicants, narcotics, licentiousness, profanity, vulgarity, disorder, and anything that might subject me to reproach or censure within or without the college.

To be diligent in my academic studies and in my military training. To do nothing inconsistent with my status as a cadet.

To take pride in my uniform and in the noble traditions of the college and never do anything that would bring discredit upon them.

To be courteous and professional in my deportment, bearing, and speech, and to exhibit good manners on all occasions.

To cultivate dignity, poise, affability, and a quiet and firm demeanor. To make friends with refined, cultivated, and intellectual people.

To improve my mind by reading and participation in intellectual and cultural activities.

To keep my body healthy and strong by physical exercise and participation in many sports.

To be generous and helpful to others and to endeavor restrain them from doing wrong.

To face difficulties with courage and fortitude and not to complain or be discouraged.

To be worthy of the sacrifices of my parents, the generosity of the state, and the efforts of all who teach and all who administer the college in order that I might receive an education and to recognize my obligation to them.

To make the college better by reason of my being a cadet.

To resolve to carry its standards into my future career and to place right above gain and a reputation for integrity above power.

To remember always that the honor of being a Citadel Cadet and graduate imposes upon me a corresponding obligation to live up to this code.

GEN. CHARLES P. SUMMERALL
U.S. ARMY, RETIRED, PRESIDENT 1931-1953

*****

NOTE: The foregoing code is earnestly commended to all cadets as an interpretation of the ideals of The Citadel.

*"The Citadel Code" was devised by World War I*
*General Charles P. Summerall.*
*Its precepts are timeless.*

Indeed, the unique standing that the college has achieved may be defined by the four years of the cadet experience. However, it is the individual graduates who raise the value of the ring far beyond the weight of its gold. They exhibit initiative, sacrifice, resolve—and timely leadership when the situation requires one to step forward. The "code" of being a cadet remains always.

# Section Four:
# Self-Actualization

Perhaps it's best that the past never become passé. There is much to contribute. There are values to discern across the years. The forays into the social norms become the laboratory for the lessons gained years before. There is a sense that we all grow into ourselves through our knowledge, our intuition, and our experiences. Our self-actualization is never a moment, but rather a series of moments that move rapidly together like the frames in a reel of film.

We have the opportunity to set examples and influence others. We will all encounter situations that might lead those with lesser character reinforcement to make unethical decisions. We have occasions to reemphasize our convictions— and some of these learning examples can occur in the presence of young minds who will benefit from our actions and perhaps follow our example.

We take what we have learned and are subtly empowered to share when called upon.

# *Mentoring Elements*

What gives us the right to mentor? Age? Experience? Perhaps it may be that we "Old Corps" folks have already made all of the mistakes. Mistakes are the most memorable teachers.

There is always an element of ***mentorship*** that makes a difference. Mentors can make every life better. Those mentored become advocates of passing it on to others—"paying it forward." Mentorship is an attitude of being there when needed. The Citadel graduate, especially, seems to promote this groundswell attitude of reaching out to assist others. The mentorship dynamic should never be understated.

There are unanticipated rewards beyond the simple act of helping someone. The Class of 2000 produced USAF Major Tevan Green. His post-Air Force career vaulted him to business prominence and the selection from the National Jaycees (Junior Chamber of Commerce) as one of "Ten Outstanding Young Americans" in 2014. Previously, this award had gone to John F. Kennedy, Dick Cheney, Wayne Newton, LaToya Jackson, Kurt Warner, Gale Sayers, and Elvis Presley.[54] Tevan grew up in Charleston and made his way to The Citadel by his determination to have an opportunity to succeed. As someone who deeply cared about his progress, I was quite proud that he invited me to an elegant ceremony in Baltimore for deserving young people. Tevan later served on The Citadel Foundation Board of Directors.

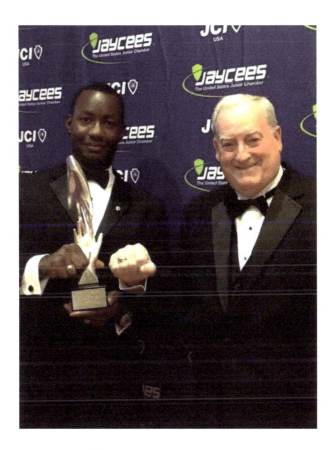

*Class of 2000 graduate Tevan Green was selected nationally*
*as one of the Ten Outstanding Young Americans.*
*Photo by Brenda Green.*

Mentorship is an active alumni privilege by which the seeds flourish and beget other secondary growth. Tevan Green has become an exceptional mentor to many others.

"I have had the privilege of those who reached out to help me when I was young and inquisitive. When I could have veered to so many distractions, there were hands to lift me up and to inspire me to accomplish long term goals. Those help-ing hands are why I find so much passion in paying it forward and helping others like those who have helped me," Green stated. "The Citadel is a special place. It's where a chosen and productive course of a lifetime can be charted."

Tevan Green rose through Air Force ranks until a training accident broke his back. Medically discharged, he used his Citadel skills to begin his own company, Citadel Logic LLC of Hampton, Virginia. This integrated business solutions company has thrived under his direction.

His four-year experience became the template for organizing and directing his career.

We would be quite fortunate to have access to highly successful celebrity mentors, but that would be a rare circumstance. Can we check with a Wall Street baron about a potential investment, or text a Nobel Laureate with an invention idea? That's not likely. But we can reach out to those who are in our growing sphere of influence. These may be relatives, teachers, religious leaders, or co-workers. They may also be members of the extensive network of Citadel alumni whom we have yet to meet.

It's easy to determine your particular mentorship team. Here's a seven-step mentor identification template:

1. Name someone you particularly enjoy being around for their conversational abilities and keen insights.

2. Who was your most admired and sage teacher pre-college? There was someone who may have taken a special interest in your development.

3. Is there a friend or a trusted expert you would call first if you needed financial advice? Add this person to your mentorship catalog.

4. Which family member has always given you the best insight? This is a great source from a "pod" that has known you forever! Normally a parent would fill this role – but it could be an aunt or an uncle.

5. Is there a professor or academic advisor from college or even someone from your fledgling career that you trust more than others?

6. Is there someone else in your life that often makes you feel special? This could be someone you met in a civic environment or socially.

7. Is there a person you know whom you wouldn't hesitate to tell any secret...a confidant? Often, this is your spouse or best friend.

There you have it. We've discovered your mentorship team! And you may wish to add even more qualified counselors. What makes your mentorship team special is that you have a relationship. They would be honored to know how much you value them and would be delighted if you called or visited. These mentoring influences may or may not have a wide public distinction. But they do have familiarity and, likely a pleasant interest in you.

*The people who make a difference in your life are not the ones with the most credentials, the most money ... or the most awards. They simply are the ones who care the most.*[55]

Similarly, you may be within a young person's circle of mentors. It may be your children or grandchildren, people beginning a career you have mastered, or young adults seeking key insights you already know. What you know from experience becomes what you are happy to impart for another's benefit.

Being a mentor is an honor based on trust. One earns the mentorship status by exemplary standards best outlined in what it takes to live honorably and ethically.

## *Courtesies, Manners, and Conduct*

At the risk of being cited as prudish or haughty, there is another product of The Citadel's experience that should be addressed for its timely impact upon all of society. The college demands proper decorum. There is a right way, and it must be followed. Too often we fall into the routine of ambivalence with a touch of ugly vulgarity.

What separates basic human decency from the barbarianism of centuries past? What do we expect of our private and public interaction—our standard of conduct? When it is okay to dispense with "Yes sir; no sir; no excuse, sir (or ma'am)?" Is our civility negotiable?

Should we expect more from ourselves? Let's start with proper communication. Training in human interaction, at The Citadel or elsewhere, has no course in invective-laden phraseology. It has no place in polite society.

Over a generation or more, the media, the movies, and maybe even the backyard fence have witnessed social exchanges that have settled into the eruption of expletive-laced dialogue. Many profane terminologies have entered the public domain as if to be socially acceptable these days. Words that would incite a bar of soap for a mouth-washing just a generation ago are now coined as routine everyday descriptions. Guttural words are tossed around in mixed company and in front of young children as if even the children were expected to adopt the habit. What happened? These brazen and loud obscenities are NOT acceptable. They are vulgar. Further, those employing such epithets erroneously feel the free and public use of them as "colorful." Some would go as far as calling high profanity an art form. The coarseness of their language often promotes the pejoration of language around them. Do not fall into the trap!

Okay, we all have all slipped here and there. But that still does not make cussing and vulgar swearing a normal form of discourse. It's unbecoming and impressionable in the most negative sense.

Ostensibly, those who populate their speech with such crudeness have demonstrated that their vocabularies are bankrupt and that they have little respect for those around them. Their behavior breaches decency and makes a poor impression that often compels a reaction from those within earshot. There are thousands of exciting, descriptive, and mind-expanding proper words available. Choose the best ones that Mister Webster compiled for you that heighten your character. That practice will set you apart from the sullied masses and elevate polite conversation, the sense of mutual respect, and the academic demeanor of those engaged. The choice of ineloquent terminology is never a good one.

Language is a tool that advances mankind. Proper language upholds the sanctity of human dignity. Why denigrate it—and ourselves—with invective? Is it not beneficial to honor higher education and your personal standing by exchanging a proper level of discourse with others?

Similarly, society seems to expand and contract in the "science" of courtesy and manners. It took many centuries to develop common courtesies and expected manners. Young people were taught to stand when someone entered a room;

not to wear a hat in a building; to open doors for perfect strangers. These actions merited confidence in mankind and often engendered the smiles of those encountered.

The dearth of proper manners has become an issue left to be solved by the Millennials. Yet, we must all set the examples within the spheres of our personal behaviors.

Here are seven observations we've all experienced that occur all-too-frequently.

1. Not introducing the person with whom you arrive at a function.

2. Bringing a cell phone into a meal situation and leaving it on.

3. Not responding to invitations with RSVPs.

4. Not thanking people for their help—by example, a person giving directions, a store clerk, or a church usher.

5. Not taking the time to write a proper "Thank You" note. Handwriting is becoming an archaic practice.

6. Not arriving to appointments on time.

7. Not giving up a seat to an elderly person who is otherwise forced to stand.

There are plenty of other infractions upon accepted decency that modern society often forgets. The lack of salutations from youngsters to the older generations, blatant rudeness, interruptive conversation, inappropriate language or dress, or even the absence of proper table manners may all be approaching nadir stages. Much of the digression can be attributed to relaxed standards in the home and at lower grade levels of public education.

An incident on this point always brought a smile to our family. My father was once rudely interrupted by an expletive-speaking man seeking to find a bathroom. Being appalled at the person's belligerent approach, my dad calmly pointed the way with an answer, "It's just down at the end of the corridor to the right where the sign on the door says 'Gentlemen.' But don't let that stop you and go right on in."

A major contributor to inappropriate modern behavior patterns is the interruption of the cellphone. People become obsessed and constantly refer to their electronic devises—or even answer them and begin a conversation while at a public event or while dining companions may be waiting. Don't accept these things. These practices are bad form. They represent blatant rudeness regardless of their stated importance. The person with you is always more important than the abruption of cellular distraction.

Perhaps it is the military traditions—or even a long-held predetermination—that people are presumed to be ladies and gentlemen until proven otherwise. The Citadel sets a standard for manners, courtesies, and even proper salutations. There are no deviations from what is learned because these ameliorations to public and private living have been proven timeless. A return to the precepts of proper courtesies and manners starts with those who insist upon its appreciated level of interaction and behavior.

All of society benefits when people make the commitment to elevate others they encounter ahead of technology, haste, and narcissistic behavior.

# *Charity for All*

Charity incorporates many concepts—***tithing, empathy, selflessness, generosity,*** and ***purposeful living.*** Why would one endowed with the ability or even some degree of fortune not be charitable?

There are two schools of thought regarding charity:

1. The government will take care of those in need.

2. It is up to us.

Those who give are more inclined to give more when the need increases. The horrible COVID-19 year of 2020 bore this out.

> *Fidelity Charitable reports its clients made donations of more than $8.1 billion last year through Dec. 15—a figure that is expected to increase significantly, since 40% to 50% of annual contributions tend to be made in December. By comparison, donations in 2019 totaled $7.3 billion. Pam Norley, president of Fidelity Charitable, attributes much of the increase to the pandemic. In an August survey of almost 500 Fidelity Charitable clients, 46% said they had given more in 2020 because of the Covid crisis. Food banks and homeless shelters are among the most popular recipients, Ms. Norley*

*says. Charities that help victims of domestic violence, struggling restaurant and health-care workers, and mental-health-support groups also have been frequent recipients, philanthropy professionals say."[56]*

It seems counter-intuitive that—when people are sick and dying, and careers are on hold, or many jobs lost—charitable notions are enhanced. But the COVID-quarantined year of 2020 disproved the logic. And Citadel alumni and friends stepped forward, too. In fact, 2020 represented the second-highest fundraising year The Citadel has ever experienced—thanks to the generous spirit and steadfast support of those who recognize and seek to advance The Citadel's impact on our nation. Many other institutions reported similar surges in generosity.

The giving culture at The Citadel has enjoyed a healthy resurgence. What was once a dismal percentage of gifting graduates decades ago has become an impressive portion—now nearly 35% of Corps alumni. Giving back has become giving forward.

People give because they care. We hear the word "altruism" but are not really sure what that entails. An altruistic nature represents the pure gesture of giving without strings attached.

*They [altruists] feel that people should give to others because it's the right thing to do. While psychologists debate whether pure altruism is real, altruistic people enjoy giving and receive pleasure from the action. Many people live this value, and it's the main reason they give.*[57]

Not everyone is altruistic in the purest sense. There could be other reasons—and these, too, often result in positive achievements. Some may give for prestige or to receive a tax deduction, but their gifts go to the same good use. Professional fundraisers are adept at discerning the motivation for others to give to a charity or to better a community. They study the subject thoroughly to develop compelling "cases for philanthropic support."

*Getfullyfunded* determined that people give based on eight factors—social dynamics, altruism, trust, impact, goal proximity, overcoming difficulty, egoism, and fear of missing out.[58] There may be many reasons to give that cross-pollinate. We know that giving inspires others to give, as well.

Giving is not always a financial endeavor. The culture of giving is highly prized within the Corps of Cadets. Projects arise that may require gifts beyond funding—gifts of community service, Big Brother and Big Sister programs, and other mentoring systems of engagement. Often, it is the influence and the example of others who give that inspire charitable acts of kindness. Learning to contribute self in every form – "time, talent, and treasure" – opens avenues of benefit for every cause.

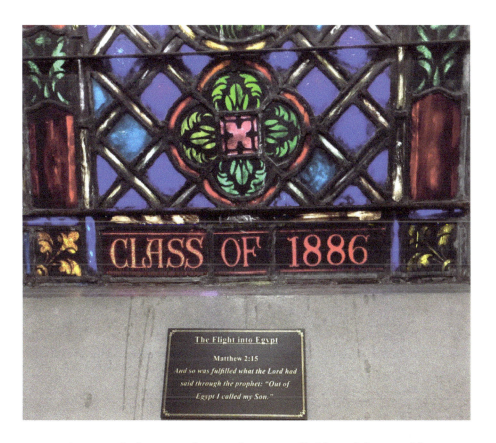

*A stained-glass window at Summerall Chapel donated by*
*The Citadel Class of 1886.*
*Giving can be a team sport that lasts well past the lives of the donors.*
*Photo by author.*

Charity is a wider concept than giving back to a college, or even providing financial support. Ostensibly, people who give often donate more than money. They donate their expertise, their spare time, and often their influence within their circles. The propensity to give of oneself is a valiant and chivalric expression. It is often done quietly, or even anonymously. It may be the quietest part of a person's inner character that finds

153

expression by sharing their blessings with others without the need for acknowledgement. This is the silent goodness seen so often "from the ranks."

Giving back seems one dimensional. It isn't. There are three types of giving. Many of us interpolate the act of giving as a call for funds that may or may not have a tax deduction benefit. What type of *generosity* is in the toolbox? Generosity is more like an adjustable wrench than a hacksaw. There are many areas of non-monetized functions.

Not all people are inclined to give. It requires one to become selfless and willing to sacrifice. We do not have to think long to conjure up examples of very wealthy entrepreneurs who became famous by their parsimonious behavior. Why is that?

Let's be empirical about giving. We can assume that some formidable number of lives will have some degree of fortune. Others will become short-circuited in that regard by economic factors, adverse health, or more pressing obligations. Those issues notwithstanding, we can assume lives of some moderate to abundant wealth accumulation, advancement of expertise in specialized service to society, and even the benefit of growing the time away from a career—leisure time—to an excess. Retirements can navigate all three of the above conditions.

There are hoarders. They save every penny, every collectible, and every asset for their own reasons. These reasons may include the unrealistic fear of running out of money and becoming destitute. There may be more incoherent protestations to the idea of charity.

It may be that the wealthy person wants to save it all for the next generation. Yet, examples of this pass-through wealth reveal countless horrible lives lived by the inherited wealth generation. These stories mirror those of an overwhelming majority of lottery winners whose lives were ruined.

Enticing children and grandchildren to live off of another's enterprising accumulation must include a heightened sense of social responsibility. There are unfortunate examples of ruined lives that may have been avoided by a sound parental strategy.

But there are also wonderful examples of this practice that warm hearts everywhere. A local billionaire and his wife focused upon his lessons to his children. Of the Jewish faith, these giving souls had their impressionable children call into a television program to outbid others for quality children's toys – toys they saw as highly desirable. These toys were then packaged and personally delivered to the poor at Christmastime. The forward-thinking parents taught them that they were part of the whole of society and that their calling was a familial responsibility to do more than others. In this way, wealth became a duty passed down effectively. Sadly, the entrepreneur died unexpectedly. But, by his poignant regard, his children grew up and became emissaries of his generous character. Their wealth, in so many ways, became a constant regenerative resource to community education. Their inspirational generosity has mattered to all.

The wealthy are also public targets. They too often become the quick solution to an organization's fundraising dilemma. For that reason, many have set up foundations to vet requests with a board of directors who may require stringent guidelines for consideration.

Giving is not always a financial enterprise.

A second avenue of giving is by sharing one's expertise within a cause. It may be that a retired optometrist may be limited in the ability to financially assist to the poor but may be able to spend a day each week to perform eye exams at a community center. The same could be said for a brick mason or a landscaper. Utilizing one's talent to help others may supersede the need for funding. Thus, there is "sweat equity" to be considered in fundraising. Could an organization's goal to fund three professional positions be minimized by recruiting three retired volunteers who mirror the expertise needed?

But what if one has no specific area of expertise? They can contribute by the third area of generosity. They can give of their time. That time could be used to set up a water purification system at a religious mission in Central America or assist in the construction of a residence for a disabled military veteran. It could be as simple as giving of time at a soup kitchen for the needy. When one donates one's time, then that time becomes the donation itself.

As giving is truly its own reward, the world around us becomes less and less hardened by vice, cruelty, poverty, and greed.

# On Patriotism

There seems to be a forgotten sense of what it means to be an American. After all, we came up with the best system of government the world has ever known. We invented a system that best suits every condition of humanity—the constitutional republic. That form did not arrive capriciously. And we defended it so often that those who were injured or even died with selfless valor are our highest order of citizens—patriots.

What happened to patriotism?

Colonized English subjects opposed the world's most powerful monarchy for reasons that were so significant in their grievance that tens of thousands were killed, wounded, or captured. Nearly 17,000 of the "Continentals" died in captivity, an astounding number given the times.[59] One of every twenty patriots died in the "American Cause" during the eight-year Revolutionary War.[60] By comparison, less than one half of one percent of all age-eligible Americans serve in today's military.[61]

The American Revolution was an excruciating birth to attain self-rule. The U.S. Constitution and Bill of Rights ensued. Much was devoted to the operational integrity of the new nation, while other emphasis was placed upon the rights of citizens. The best documents known to exist were considered from the *Magna Carta* (King John at Runnymede in 1215) to *The Fundamental Constitutions of Carolina* (John Locke, March 1, 1669).[62]

Incredibly, young people know very little of the history, reasoning, and application of these documents. It may be because our public educational system has emphasized STEM courses (science, technology, engineering and mathematics) during the last few decades over geography, history, and civics. There are myriad other explanations. But the result is troubling. There are those who foist other forms of governance that are the antithesis of a constitutional republic. Though the failures of alternative governance have ruined untold lives and ravaged nations, their carcasses are dug up again and again. The anarchist, fascist, communist, and socialist dialogues present ideologies fraught with failure. Millions have fled these countries over the last century. Yet the systems, especially socialism, are reintroduced as if they were new ideals to correct perceived issues of income, property, and social inequalities. The middle school history and civics lessons are sorely missed.

> *It can easily be argued that America's most important export has been the Constitution of the United States. It was the first single-document constitution. It is the longest-lived. And in only two centuries, virtually every nation has come to accept the inevitability and value of having a constitution. This fact transcends differences of culture, history, and legal heritage. The United States Constitution is perceived as the fundamental point of reference, even by regimes whose philosophical outlook is antidemocratic. Furthermore, nearly every nation has accepted the "Philadelphia formula"—either*

*internally or universally—as the means by which an effective constitution can best be produced.*[63]

France was the first post-American-Revolution country to embrace the idea of the rights of man and societal liberty. The French Revolution of 1789 changed the course of that nation's history. The French citizenry roiled against the ruling class, the lack of individual rights, and other oppressions. The French saw the success of the Americans firsthand as our most beneficial ally against the British just a decade earlier.

**The entrance to Lesesne Gate is mindful of a military base though the public is universally welcomed.**
**Photo by author.**

Ten years later, the Irish suffered a failed revolution, the Irish Rebellion of 1799. But they did not lose sight of their objective and gained independence from the British as the Irish Free State in 1922. Many other countries began to see the most advanced system of governance the world has known. Even monarchal Great Britain saw the benefit and adopted a similar tri-power system, albeit with more political parties. The monarchy became a symbolic vestige of the past.

Civilization changed because of America.

The American system of governance has stood the test of time. It stands as the longest and most envied system extant.

> *The United States was the first nation to have an elected head of state called a president. It was a constitutionally created president, described by Harold J. Laski as "both more and less than a king; both more and less than a prime minister."[64] Today more than half the world's nations have presidents as their chief executives, some with even more constitutional power than the American president (France, South Africa), many with only nominal ceremonial powers (India, Zimbabwe). The American Constitution formalized the concepts required to make such a system work: the separation of powers and the system of checks and balances. The result balances leadership and minimizes abuse, encourages stability and obviates tyranny.[65]*

Yet there are those who condemn the U.S. Constitution, the rule of law, and even the business of business—capitalism.

These detractors range from the under-informed, the misinformed, and the ideologues to an even more sinister group—those who want to destroy the American way of life. They want to forcibly impose hybrid mixtures of all the governing failures that lie on the scrapheap of history. The growth in that last sector—especially among the Millennials—has become startling. Informed citizens know better. Patriotism should forever be embraced by the tenets that gave its rise.

*The U.S. Navy's Blue Angels fly in formation over*
*The Citadel Campus.*
*Photo provided by The Citadel Archives.*

What happened to our history? It seems we have lowered its relevance to the point of more recent blatant denigration. Is it because our history is not good? Not all history is good.

But it is all there—and it was taught to be truthful and a template for betterment. Too many college-age students have no idea how government works, how our constitution protects citizens, or what sacrifices so many patriots have made to provide the freedoms we enjoy. We must reach back to our founding principles so that our future can be realized.

Likely because of the military training component, cadets at The Citadel better understand the sacrifices made to preserve and protect our citizens and our way of life—especially our liberty and our freedom. The specter of patriotism arises. From time to time, those who value these regenerative American concepts are called upon—and they respond bravely as patriots to the cause. Make no mistake, our country was born from the blood of selfless and loyal patriots.

Education is always the answer. There is a responsibility to have one's voice heard at local, statewide, and national elections. We should understand social and economic issues, know our founding documents, and the systems of checks and balances that make our form of government unique and effective. Being American should inspire the virtue of patriotism. It was patriotism that made us Americans.

# *A Word About Humility*

There was a crash course in **humility** that every cadet experienced. Whether a cadet recruit to the plebe system was a high school valedictorian, the football captain, or the homecoming queen a few months earlier, these quieted souls were in some state of awe when they reported to their company first sergeant for the first time. The elevator from the penthouse to the basement was swift. All were humbled.

The haughty and the arrogant—the narcissistic and the self-important—were brought to the commonality of a new baseline. They were tossed upon the "sea of nobodies." They were lowly plebes in a system meant to build upon a new character immersed in humility.

As experience grew and the tiny steps of accomplishment nurtured each, there was no room for selfishness, conceit, or overconfidence. Careful interaction with others, adherence to duty and cause, and the new reliance upon trust and teamwork emerged. The plight of character was built upon new and proven foundations. While confidence became a result, it was a journey meant for both personal fortitude and mentoring influence. Nobody does it alone. It makes the ring more valuable by its toil and circumstance. A cadet was broken down into essential parts and put back together like one would perform in re-assembling a rifle. And like that rifle, the egotism was oiled away. Humility found its place.

Humility is perhaps the most refreshing part of any person. How many times have we met military heroes, best-selling authors, or high profile and accomplished business personalities to find that they do not place themselves above others? They are more likely to ask questions about your stead in life. What stands out in others is what we should internalize to ourselves. Humility is perhaps the most endearing quality we find in others.

Tongue in cheek, we sometimes earn our humility by actions that had the unintended consequence of humbling us. Humbled often enough, we may appreciate a permanent state of humility.

# Character Catalogued

## So, What Did the Ancient's Say?

How does one best live a virtuous life? We could ask psychologists, evangelists, or our mentors. The precepts of living a full and virtuous life, however, has been the conundrum of the ages. Fortunately, we have records from history. For the simplest and most straightforward approaches, we should ask the ancients. Why? Though they may have had some interruptions like war, famine, pestilence, and pandemic to survive, they didn't have the cellphone. They had more time to think!

Confucius (551-479 BCE)[66] directed common sense to character. The ancient Chinese philosopher laid out myriad timeless adages to follow. Here are three to ponder:

*There are three methods to gaining wisdom. The first is reflection, which is the highest. The second is limitation, which is the easiest. The third is experience, which is the bitterest.*

*Our greatest glory is not in never falling, but in rising every time we fall.*

*Wisdom, compassion, and courage are the three universally recognized moral qualities of men.*[67]

We can all benefit from those we recorded who lived with an adherence to the idea of stoicism—an ancient Greek avenue of philosophy that focused upon happiness and virtue.

> *Stoicism was founded at Athens by Zeno of Citium. The school taught that virtue, the highest good, is based on knowledge; the wise live in harmony with the divine Reason (also identified with Fate and Providence) that governs nature, and are indifferent to the vicissitudes of fortune and to pleasure and pain.*[68]

One would not have to know the full sentiment of the philosophy to understand the tenets expressed by its most famous followers — *Marcus Aurelius, Frederick the Great, Montaigne, George Washington, Thomas Jefferson, Adam Smith, John Stuart Mill, Theodore Roosevelt, and General James Mattis.*[69] The applications are timeless. Stoicism is relative to The Citadel experience because it is the philosophy of living purposefully in a virtuous and objective focus.

The study of Lucius Annaeus Seneca (c. 1 BCE – CE 65)[70], or simply "Seneca" reveals the simplicity. He cited that time is a non-renewable commodity that must be managed effectively and cautioned that our time is more valuable than any other item we own.[71] He preached that the way we look at death impacts the way we live. The idea that life compresses time to an uncertain period, in Seneca's explanation, underscores the critical use of time that matters daily.

*"A whole lifetime is needed to learn how to live, and—perhaps you'll find this more surprising—a whole lifetime is needed to learn how to die."[72]*

Perhaps the most popular ancient stoic quoted in history was a Roman Emperor, Marcus Aurelius (121-180).[73] Parenthetically, this emperor faced much adversity. His father died when he was three years of age.[74] He faced the terrible destruction and ensuing famine caused by the overflow of the Tiber River in Rome, several wars, the Antonine Plague which killed nearly five million, and other adversities with a sense of courage and conviction.[75] His lessons of living in virtue and justice survive by their timelessness. He wrote them down and they survive as *Meditations.*

*"At day's first light have in readiness, against disinclination to leave your bed, the thought that 'I am rising for the work of man.' Must I grumble at setting out to do what I was born for, and for the sake of which I have been brought into the world? Is this the purpose of my creations to lie here under the blankets and keep myself warm? 'Ah, but it is a great deal more pleasant!' Was it for pleasure, then, that you were born, and not for work, not for effort?"*

*"Once you have done a man a service, what more would you have? Is it not enough to have obeyed the laws of your own nature, without expecting to be paid for it? That is like the eye demanding a reward*

*for seeing, or the feet for walking. It is for that very purpose that they exist; and they have their due in doing what they were created to do. Similarly, man is born for deeds of kindness; and when he has done a kindly action, or otherwise served the common welfare, he has done what he was made for, and has received his quittance."*

*"Do not indulge in dreams of having what you have not but reckon up the chief of the blessings you do possess, and then thankfully remember how you would crave for them if they were not yours."[76]*

Living life is difficult for all of us. Nobody gets out alive! We lose our parents and other loved ones. We face health impediments. We have financial obligations. We have familial responsibilities like mentoring, feeding, and educating our children. And there is much more—often the roadblocks we do not anticipate—like the COVID-19 pandemic and economic challenges—not to mention natural disasters. Are we prepared? Can we cope?

That answer could be different within each of us. The ancient stoics adhered to a view that time is precious, relationships are special, and virtue should stand above all else.

The Greek Stoic Epictetus was able to discern that we should always live in the "now" and not concern ourselves with the past or the future. Those influences could only distort our productive time and worry because they both embodied things that either we could not change or have little impact upon changing. Recognizing what we could change in the present became an essential part of living with purpose.[77]

The Ancient Stoics advanced the idea that we should be modest yet take stock in ourselves (gain confidence) and accept ourselves for who we are with that same confidence. These lessons have made it into the third millennia. They are reestablished by experiences that cadets can learn within a disciplined framework at The Citadel.

*There are talents beyond the classroom.*
*From the Mind of Ray Mayer.*

# Postscript

Every Citadel career seems to have a heartfelt story of re-demption, resilience, or perseverance. Citadel cadets became Citadel citizens and took what they learned to other parts of society where their significance mattered. Though the law of large numbers over a pool of nearly 39,000 living graduates would indicate some missteps and failures, by-and-large, the cadet graduate has a solid history of success. We have ferreted out into all fields—federal judges, business owners, professors, astronauts, entrepreneurs, athletes, musicians, engineers, politicians, and pastors. There are architects and authors, inventors, doctors, and analysts. The Citadel's wide academic offerings have set in motion the goals of a purposeful life.

The base nature of a graduate is to forge an enterprise of life that becomes consistent with the precepts learned in those four short years. Lifelong friendships are earned, and there is a clear path that employs the value of discipline to a purpose. One has the ability to attain life's goals within the guidelines of that standard. Then there is also a *Blue Book of Life* beyond the *Blue Book* every cadet was issued as a "cadet recruit."

Cadet graduates have these tools as well as distractions that often take them away from what was ingrained. We are as susceptible as anyone to veer from the chartered course. But what we have experienced gives a clear view of the path forward. It is up to us to adhere to the lessons learned.

By the assessment provided annually by The Citadel Foundation, the modern campus thrives. The following set of general "State of the College" statistics are from the academic year 2020-2021.

Today's Citadel has benefits that were quite rare a half-century ago. For instance, 85% of the cadet population receives some amount of financial assistance, most (70%) by way of donor-funded scholarships.[78] The growth of The Citadel Foundation has been a healthy contributor to the college's national standing. The nearly 40% of The Citadel's out-of-state student population has a four-year tuition bill that approximates $200,000. The capability to defray much of these costs has been a catalyst of quality as each year's entering class seems to push the average cadet SAT score higher.

The college continues vigorously to recruit females and minorities. The minority population in the Corps of Cadets has grown to 23%, while the female population that had been below 10% for the first twenty years of co-education (begun earnestly in 1996) reached 13% by 2021.[79]

Though funding has grown in the private-donor sector, all institutions of higher education in South Carolina continue to struggle from the lack of state support, especially in the areas of capital improvements and deferred maintenance. Historically, The Citadel's percentage of state support provided toward its roughly $150 million annual budget has fallen below ten percent. The trend has continued over the previous two decades. The conundrum of the shrinking support is that the State of South Carolina General Assembly also rules over the tuition increases that are often necessary to balance the school's budget. Despite these facts, the college has been ever adaptive in creating new ways to survive and thrive. Donors have made the largest impact. Executive leadership from the college president, the administration, the Board of Visitors, and The Citadel Foundation has been acutely necessary and has delivered.

The college has independently executed its vision to provide resources, mentorship, and adaptive programs to prepare graduates to serve a changing world while carrying the banner of principled leadership. The Citadel Foundation has placed a relatively new emphasis upon endowing the future by way of named scholarships and unique cadet programs—especially in the areas of ethics and leadership. By the foresight of leveraging perpetual endowments, The Citadel is able to navigate the future by drawing upon the experiences of past graduates. The myriad programs and scholarships resulting from these endowed funds are harbingers of what will come. Like the individual cadet who finds a way to succeed against the challenges of barracks' life, The Citadel will prevail.

# *Esprit de Corps*

The Corps of Cadets is unique among institutions of higher learning. Cadets stick together. One finds that the Corps often acts as one—from top down and bottom up. When one cadet experiences medical distress or financial straits, the Corps becomes a family. There seems to be at least one occasion in every cadet's experience where the Corps rallied to a cause greater than self.

A collective arrangement of Corps spirit can be seen on six Saturdays in the fall. The football Bulldogs compete on the gridiron and the Corps can be counted upon to pull them through to victory. The public is invited each Friday afternoon for a dress parade performance by the South Carolina Corps of Cadets and its rousing marching band. Be ready for the cannon fire!

*The 2006-2008 renovated Johnson Hagood Stadium home side*
*is a state-of-the-art facility.*
*The new artificial turf covers Sansom Field and*
*is uniquely cited as "The Boneyard."*

Cadet interaction is encouraged as friendships coalesce. The Corps spirit can be seen at social events like senior class parties, but there are many more profound examples. The support of the Corps becomes evident when a cadet loses a parent, or experiences a serious auto accident, or in those life-changing moments when word arrives that a recent graduate has paid the ultimate sacrifice in combat. These are the times when the Corps rallies to the aid of an individual who needs the support to get through a crisis. They become brothers and sisters in arms, and they show ardent support for one another.

It is in the toolbox to every cadet that some form of co-hesion is in demand.  This condition presents a ***teamwork*** psychology.  It occurs when someone does a little extra work to build the consensus and recruit others to a cause, to an action, or to gather needed funds.  It is within the auspices of the *Esprit de Corps* that cadets form alliances of support to achieve a result for others—often anonymously.  And that sentiment does not evaporate at graduation.

Cadet graduates come back to remember—to feel the presence of others who have been a part of their cadet experience. They see the campus, though much has changed, in the warm soup of nostalgia.  They remember.

*The Swain Family Boating Center gives a screened porch view of the Ashley River.*
*Photo by author.*

Interviews with current cadets—in this case, those from the Corps of 2020-2021—reveal that much of what may have been true fifty years ago may still be around fifty years hence.

For example, several sentiments expressed that the "Corps Squad" athletes had it easier than the rest of the Corps. Yet, few members of the Corps of Cadets would take the time to attend a football or basketball practice to witness the extraordinary conditioning and mental toughness required to compete at the NCAA level. The rest of the Corps has the attitude that the "jocks" get out of parade and drill. In recent years, there has been more energy and expertise devoted to closing these misperceptions, and the Corps is more unified as a result.

The overwhelming backlash during this particular landmark year in the Corps has been the cadet attitude associated with a nuance deemed as the "Sophomore Shuffle." This Jenkins Hall program began with the returning sophomores in academic year 2020-2021. These cadets were each reassigned to new companies to balance the cadet population and discourage other pejorative company activities. The idea is to curb hazing and to improve the avenues of cadet leadership. The plan has been fraught with controversy from its inception, though generally considered a plan for the improvement of the overall cadet leadership system.

From a practical standpoint, the sophomores in the 2020-2021 class year abhor the change. In speaking with several sophomore cadets, they feel as if their entire class has been offered in sacrifice to a failed experiment. Further complicating the experiment, the sophomores reported to their newly assigned companies under COVID-19 social distancing protocols under which they could not interact with their new classmates for the better part of the fall semester. They were not allowed to interact with their upper-class cadets or company academic advisors in battalion during ESP. Incoming freshmen were housed together in separate battalions, so the sophomores were forced to resume the sweep details and other subservient duties they expected to have terminated after completing their freshman year.

One female cadet noted that she returns to her "knob year company" daily to visit while finding it hard to acclimate herself to the "sophomore shuffle" company, where she hardly knows anyone. When asked about the general *Esprit de Corps*, she noted that the shuffle has become a universal Corps morale changer that all factions hope will lessen in time. She even noted that as a volunteer at The Citadel's call center, she has had many hang-up calls from disgruntled alumni over their resilience of the shuffle system. Yet, like all around her, she is adjusting. The interruption of the COVID-19 protocols could make the transition more difficult for the administration and the cadets, as well.

Perhaps the "Sophomore Shuffle" dilemma will become less volatile as time weathers its introduction. Particularly in a place defined by tradition, change is always difficult and often controversial. Time heals.

Conversely, the Corps has had several opportunities to fuse as one. The daily lives of cadets foster a teamwork attitude. There are community service functions that have inspired the Corps to participate and to take pride in the results. Even the movement of sophomore cadets presents opportunities as experiences broaden and the circle of classmate relationship bonds swell. More adjustment may be in order from concerned alumni –who have always been factored into decisions related to tradition, effectiveness, betterment, and the promotion of "principled leadership in an academic environment."

# A Collage of Today's Citadel

A walk-through of The Citadel's pristine campus shows that though much has not changed, change is most certainly prevalent. Much of what was old and dilapidated is gone – Thompson Hall, the former boat house, the red brick football stadium, the former national guard armory, and much more. There are no keypunch machines or pay phone locations. A new War Memorial was added, spearheaded by The Citadel Class of 1967. McAlister Field House was updated with new seats, flooring and an impressive scoreboard—courtesy of the Class of 1964. Locker rooms were modernized and added. A cadet indoor rifle range borders WLI Field near the marsh. Coward Hall has been updated and expanded. Cadets can select from a buffet inside during two meal shifts. The college has adapted to the world around us. The course offerings suggest the same and business and industry demand more specialized abilities to fill need.

The following pages are meant to bring the visual of the college back into focus for the alumni base—especially those who have other obligations or travel hardships that make it difficult to return. As your company supply sergeant may have reported, "All is in order and accounted for, sir!"

*By conjecture, the pranked messages painted over the years on The Citadel's water tower have made the layers of paint more prevalent than that of the Golden Gate Bridge.*

# *Returning to the Moments*80

*Roll onto the ground expanse*
*And hear the PT chants*
*Behold the jet in its napping*
*Or listen to the river lapping*
*The tank restrained sits vacant*
*The oak lanes sleep adjacent*
*Roll into the barracks parquet*
*To roll out and roll away*
*There's a back hill that climbs*
*To the sense of rigorous times*
*And the carillon rings out*
*Near those war dead devout*
*With a cadence encore, we may*
*Roll out and then roll away*
*To return to those days of yore*
*Recall that* Esprit de Corps.
*And by a courteous head bow*
*For the past has become the now*
*Where God demands we heed the truth*
*"To Remember Now Thy Creator in the Days of Thy Youth."*81

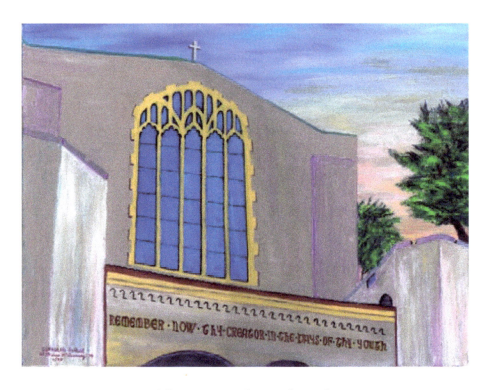

*The Message Carried Forth.*
*Oil on Canvas by Author.*

# The Visual Satire...
## Cartoons Portraying Cadet Life

The prevalent inside humor of a military campus may not register with those who have no idea of The Citadel as basically a closed community. The Citadel is much like a cloister or a monastery, though our "novices" talk even less! The central element to the vest pocket humor is the cartoons that would run bi-weekly in the campus newspaper, *The Brigadier*.

There was no better cartoonist than the amazing Ray Mayer, who served as Oscar Company Executive Officer. Mayer's career was not as a cartoonist, but as a lawyer and prosecutor. He became a published author with the introduction of his riveting 2018 novel, *From Valor, Triumph*. He was kind enough to reach into his magic mind and provide even more hilarity well past his last *Brigadier* deadline.

To understand the humor, one would need to understand the factions on campus—the tactical officers, the administration, the commandant, the regimental staff, the athletic "Corps Squad," the cadet laundry, Coward Hall activities (mess hall), the Bond Volunteers, those posting *Dear John* letters, and especially what happens outside the walls (cadets' comportment on general leave). There are other events and topics for the insular humor—the classroom, Corps Day, Homecoming, PT (physical training), Saturday Morning Inspections, senior class parties, cadet intramural contests, and parade. Subject matter for the Corps of Cadets remains fertile for satire.

Here are a few timeless cartoons, courtesy of Ray Mayer:

185

*Being a bit startled by a surprise inspection
never reduced the punishment.*

*Some roommates studied the fine art of wrestling
during Evening Study Period.*

*An Alumni pilot's flyover revenge…*

*Saturday Morning Protocol: "Remember, those who write the most white slips wins."*

*Cadet Private Roland gained a new attitude about life by Christmas.*

*"You're making an excellent choice, pal.
Where you come from, we're a piece 'a cake."*

## *Positive Human Consequence*

On a personal note, when I was a sophomore, I bought a used and discounted store-display portable typewriter with what little money I had ($39). It was essential to support the classroom requirements of my chosen major—English. In time, I would recoup that full expense by a multiple simply by typing other's ERWs and term papers at yeoman's pricing. That cheap typewriter became my ally in solidifying my academic career. I saw it as my door to the future after college. But that element did not present itself until many years later.

In my post-Citadel years, I had prioritized paying back my student loans to the point that I passed over a journalism career—an avenue that better suited my skills. My decision to pursue a less-desirable pathway made me more financially responsible. Looking back, it was that Citadel pedigree that vaulted me through the early interviews past other very capable candidates. Yes, the ring made a difference and more than doubled the salary I would have made when offered a career as a newspaper journalist. My personal conundrum in the weeks leading to graduation was that I had offers from several publications that I could not afford to accept! But I never gave up on my dreams of getting back to what first motivated me as a cadet—journalism. The mentorship of those selfless professors in the Department of English provided the tools. This, my fifteenth book, is as much a credit to them as it would be to my parents, my wife, and other mentoring influences who motivated me to return to my passion.

*Imagine the toil of typing!*

That vintage Smith Corona Corsair Deluxe Aqua Blue Portable Typewriter is long gone—replaced by an Apple Mac that has the same letters on its keyboard in all the same places. My oversized fingers seem to strike the right keys, and the program will often self-correct some misplaced commas and bonehead spellings or introduce some hilarious new ones. Perhaps it was propitious that I returned to my journalistic roots after those advances saved me from carbon paper and *Wite-Out*. And the Daniel Library's Dewey Decimal System has faded into the mist, much like the teaching of Latin or the Palmer Method of handwriting. The world has advanced across every facet of learning. Perhaps it's apocryphal that The Citadel has taken its rightful place on the mantle of humanity. That experience emanates always.

We make our own way. We seek, we learn, and we react. In my own "look-back" experience, I saw that there were lessons I could leave for my children and grandchildren. These lessons were gleaned from the experience of living—and observing. Over the years I took the time to jot these inspirations down and place them in an old used gift box. The box was stored away at my office. When I rediscovered that box recently, I decided to re-assemble the motivational notes contained therein. They gave me an insight to my self-invented acronym—the PHC—or ***Positive Human Consequence***. There are well-intended thoughts and simple courtesies that could make a difference to someone who may need a timely enhancement of life.

Simply stated, our ***positive human consequence*** is the reason we exist. What are we each bringing to the table? What will we leave to others? How can we improve the world around us, if even by inches and ounces?

Here's the PHC listing from a half-century of inspirational observations:

1. Always stoop to see into children's eyes at the equal height of the world in which they live. It prioritizes them and brings you back to an innocence of things you never imagined.

2. Make trauma internal to the degree that it does not lessen the optimism of others. It is the most selfless gesture you can offer.

3. Engage in communication with someone you haven't spoken to in a year or more. It matters both to you and to that person. Friends, family, and acquaintances recharge us.

4. Listen to your emotions. Tears come from both sadness and happiness. They are the mortar of mankind.

5. Open and clear views never include the spot where you're standing. Imagine another's perspective before making your opinion known.

6. Humble and sincere service to humanity is the only antidote to the sin of arrogance.

7. Imagine how your triumphs could benefit others. Your good fortune brings an opportunity to enhance another's happiness, as well. Share happiness always.

8. Never find excuses to give up. The light behind the next door may be celestial.

9. Share a quiet sunset. That simple joy is greater than all the world's riches.

10. Unsolicited acts of anonymous and spontaneous charity will move your soul beyond earth's aura.

11. It is timeless to lend your most cherished asset to a stranger in need—your smile. It could disrupt the coldness of life's shadow. Smiles may come back tenfold.

12. Bring dreams to life. All art, culture, design, and science grew from dreams that dreamers dreamt. Share dreams into reality. Then, dream your next dream.

13. Prayer works. The fact that there is prayer offered always makes adversity tenable. Prayer is the strongest silence known.

14. Laugh. And then laugh again. Laughter makes your heart leap beyond the bounds of gravity. Laughter is the best remedy for every malady known.

15. And from Ecclesiastes 12:1 (KJV), - the inscription on Summerall Chapel- "Remember Now Thy Creator in the Days of Thy Youth." God will never leave you.

# About the Author

## W. Thomas McQueeney, Cadet #58964

*Author W. Thomas McQueeney, '74, receives the Henry J. Taylor*
*Cup Literary Award,*
*Presented by the President of The Citadel,*
*General James W. Duckett.*

W. Thomas McQueeney graduated from The Citadel in 1974 to pursue a career in finance and financial planning. Over the last forty years, he has served as a State Farm insurance agent within the Charleston metro area. The author is the fourth of nine children, six of whom graduated from The Citadel. He majored in English and distinguished himself as an honor graduate, Dean's List student, and Sports Editor of *The Brigadier*. He was awarded multiple journalistic accolades relative to his contributions within The Citadel's English Department, *The Brigadier*, and *The Shako*. An Oscar Company cadet, he served on Fourth Battalion Staff as a senior.

McQueeney's commitments to the community, the State of South Carolina, and the nation have accorded him the *Order of the Palmetto*, the highest civilian award rendered by the State of South Carolina. He serves as the Chairman of the Congressional Medal of Honor Museum Foundation, a $55 million project that will host the national offices of the Congressional Medal of Honor Society. The National Medal of Honor Leadership and Education Center will house The Congressional Medal of Honor Museum and a national education program featuring ethics, valor, patriotism, and selflessness.

His dedication to The Citadel includes considerable active support, to include more than thirty years of service as the Class of 1974 TCF Chairman. He chaired the $44.5 million renovation of Johnson Hagood Stadium (2003-2008). He served the college as a member of The Citadel Foundation Board of Directors (2005-2013) and The Citadel Board of Visitors (2006-2012). He is an honorary member of The Citadel Athletic Hall of Fame and became a legacy donor to the college as a member of The Citadel's Society of 1842. His other Citadel activities include service on boards to renovate the stained-glass windows at Summerall Chapel, The Citadel Athletic Hall of Fame board, and the Ralph H. Johnson Medal of Honor Scholarship Committee. He founded The Citadel Fastbreak Club in 1984 and served as chairman of the Southern Conference Basketball Championships.

McQueeney founded Santa's Kind Intentions in 1998, an organization that provides for the needy at Christmas. He has served as Grand Knight of Knights of Columbus Council 704, a Catholic fraternal order whose purpose is charity. It is the largest council in South Carolina. He also served as Race Director of the K of C Turkey Day Run, the largest 5K race in South Carolina. The author served with others to form One New Humanity Charleston in 2021, an organization among churches that advocates new social and religious interaction to sew together divisions of faith, race, and economic strata. It is a peace through prayer initiative.

McQueeney has chaired or served on the board of directors of more than two dozen other community, statewide, and national boards.

The author has published fourteen other books across various genres to include histories, biographies, travel, literary offerings, humor, and a novel. McQueeney has four children and five grandchildren. He and his wife, Amanda, live in Mount Pleasant.

*Cheers!*
*A salute to the membership of The Citadel's Board of Visitors.*
*Author's Board Tribute Dinner 2012.*
*Photo by Amanda McQueeney.*

# Endnotes

1 General information obtained from The *Citadel.edu* Website with additional information supplied by the research and personal experience of the author. Also compiled from https://www.britannica.com/topic/The-Citadel-college-South-Carolina.

2 Governor Richardson quote. https://www.citadel.edu/root/brief-history.

3 Civil War death toll. https://www.battlefields.org/learn/articles/civil-war-casualties

4 President Franklin D. Roosevelt. https://www.presidency.ucsb.edu/documents/remarks-the-citadel-charleston-south-carolina-0

5 Citadel losses in Civil War. https://www.citadel.edu/root/brief-history.

6 Story of the Class that Never Was. https://www.citadel.edu/root/class-never-was-four-languages

7 Charles Foster. https://www.citadel.edu/root/brief-history.

8 Name change. https://www.citadel.edu/root/brief-history.

9 The Citadel Beach House History. https://www.citadel.edu/root/beachclub-history

10 Arland D. Williams, Jr. https://today.cita.del.edu/remembering-air-florida-flight-90-hero-arland-williams-jr-citadel-class-of-1957/

11 Lt. Col. Charles D. Hodges. https://today.citadel.edu/citadel-graduate-involved-in-thai-cave-rescue-describes-dramatic-operation/

12 Vietnam War deaths. https://www.britannica.com/event/Vietnam-War

13 Citadel Casualties Vietnam. http://www.citadel.edu/citadel-history/war-deaths.html

14 Lt. Gen. John W. Rosa Jr. https://www.postandcourier.com/news/lt-gen-john-rosa-looks-back-on-12-years-as-citadel-president/article_2b04a05a-1d97-11e8-bc39-a34bf4953f1c.html

15 Bill Krause Quote. Provided by The Citadel Foundation.

16 Citadel Alumni Association. http://www.citadelalumni.org/s/1674/images/gid1001/editor_documents/about/bylaws.pdf?gid=1001&pgid=61

17 World sprint record 1891. https://www.liveabout.com/mens-100-meter-world-records-3259154

18 Usain Bolt. https://www.olympicchannel.com/en/stories/features/detail/usain-bolt-record-world-champion-athlete-fastest-man-olympics-sprinter-100m-200m/

19 Marathon record. https://www.worldathletics.org/news/report/berlin-marathon-2018-eliud-kipchoge-world-rec

20 Human Capacity. https://www.streetdirectory.com/travel_guide/8323/self_improvement_and_motivation/17_extraordinary_human_capacities.html

21 Letter to son by Robert E. Lee. https://www.historynet.com/mexican-war-the-proving-ground-for-future-american-civil-war-generals.htm

22 Two-Parent Households. https://www.washingtonpost.com/news/wonk/wp/2014/09/08/children-with-married-parents-are-better-off-but-marriage-isnt-the-reason-why/

23 Duty in a Democracy. https://www.americanbar.org/groups/crsj/publications/human_rights_magazine_home/we-the-people/civic-duties-civil-virtues/

24 Freshman Time Management. https://www.citadel.edu/root/rotc

25 College ranking Honesty. https://www.collegemagazine.com/cms-top-10-most-honest-colleges/

26 Washington Post on Honor Codes. https://www.washingtonpost.com/posteverything/wp/2015/05/28/why-colleges-should-ditch-honor-codes/

27 Anonymous honor. https://www.artofmanliness.com/articles/manly-honor-vi-the-decline-of-traditional-honor-in-the-west-in-the-20th-century/

28 Internet lying. https://www.ted.com/talks/jeff_hancock_the_future_of_lying?referrer=playlist-5_talks_on_the_truth_about_lyi

29 The Citadel Blue Book. https://www.citadel.edu/root/images/commandant/blue-book.pdf

30 Pat Conroy. https://www.postandcourier.com/features/arts_and_travel/pat-conroy-s-literary-legacy-the-writing-life-author-conroy-battling-cancer-the-lowcountry-s/article_eb752f01-8a71-545a-9680-5a2f243f05d8.html

31 Prince of Tides. https://earlybirdbooks.com/pat-conroy

32 New York Times 2009 Harvey Schiller. https://www.nytimes.com/2009/04/20/sports/baseball/20schiller.html

33 Self-Discipline. https://www.successconsciousness.com/blog/inner-strength/self-discipline/

34 Died of Drug overdoses prior to age 30. https://www.legacy.com/news/celebrity-deaths/celebrities-who-died-before-30/

35 Chevaux de Frise. https://theodora.com/encyclopedia/c/chevauxdefrise.html

36 Orville Wright. https://www.biography.com/inventor/orville-wright

37 Chuck Yeager breaks Sound Barrier. https://www.history.com/this-day-in-history/yeager-breaks-sound-barrier

38 Chuck Yeager. IBID.

39 Shepherd. https://airandspace.si.edu/exhibitions/apollo-to-the-moon/online/early-steps/humans-in-space.cfm#:~:text=Astronaut%20Alan%20B.,186%20kilometers%20(116%20miles).

40 Trebuchet competition. https://www.reuters.com/article/us-competition-trebuchet/high-tech-medieval-weaponry-combine-in-trebuchet-competition-idUK-TRE71R0M020110228

41 Trebuchet. http://www.lordsandladies.org/trebuchet.htm

42 Creativity. https://www.forbes.com/sites/robynshulman/2020/03/10/this-is-what-happens-when-we-close-doors-on-creativity-in-the-classroom/?sh=6f9080bf151e

43 Economic Respect. https://aeon.co/essays/restoring-respect-is-the-first-step-towards-a-better-society

44 Al Gini and Ronald Green, Authors. https://www.leadershipnow.com/leading-blog/2013/06/the_ten_virtues_of_outstanding.html

45 Leadership Study. https://www.northeastern.edu/graduate/blog/top-5-leadership-qualities/

46 Medal of Honor Recipients. https://cmohmf.org/congressional-designation

47 Leadership as related to decency. https://www.mbs.net/morristown-beard-school-news/~board/news/post/basic-human-decency-and-civility-february-24-2017

48 Church attendance. https://news.gallup.com/poll/248837/church-membership-down-sharply-past-two-decades.aspx

49 Albert Einstein. https://theweek.com/articles/810619/what-einstein-thought-about-god

50 Religion on society. http://www.ohrc.on.ca/en/creed-freedom-religion-and-human-rights-special-issue-diversity-magazine-volume-93-summer-2012/relationship-between-religions-and-secular-society

51 Traditional Religion Shrinkage. https://www.pewresearch.org/fact-tank/2015/11/03/5-key-findings-about-religiosity-in-the-u-s-and-how-its-changing/

52 Justin Naylor. https://braverangels.org/the-value-of-military-service/

53 The Citadel Mission. https://www.citadel.edu/root/policies/vision,-core,-values-and-strategic-initiative

54 TOYA Awards. https://toyawards.org/toyaward/winners/toyaward/winners.aspx?likey=055a64ba-fba5-4d0b-895d-7ca9f1681fd4

55 Mentorship quote. https://livelifehappy.com/life-quotes/the-people-who-make/

56 Charitable giving 2020. https://www.wsj.com/articles/the-new-face-of-charitable-giving-during-the-pandemic-11611334800

57 Altruism. https://www.networkforgood.com/nonprofitblog/7-reasons-why-donors-give/

58 Giving. https://getfullyfunded.com/why-people-give/
59 Revolutionary War casualties. https://foxtrotalpha.jalopnik.com/
   the-revolutionary-war-by-the-numbers-1600199390
60 Percentage of male revolutionary War casualties. IBID.
61 Percentage of Americans in Military. https://fivethirtyeight.com/features/
   what-percentage-of-americans-have-served-in-the-military/
62 Fundamental Constitutions of Carolina. https://www.ncpedia.org/
   fundamental-constitutions
63 International impact of the U.S. Constitution. https://www.encyclo-
   pedia.com/politics/encyclopedias-almanacs-transcripts-and-maps/
   influence-american-constitution-abroad
64 Harold J. Laski (1893-1950) was an English-born author and professor at Harvard
   in the first half of the twentieth century.
65 American Constitution. https://www.encyclopedia.com/
   politics/encyclopedias-almanacs-transcripts-and-maps/
   influence-american-constitution-abroad
66 Confucius. https://www.britannica.com/biography/Confucius
67 Confucius Quotes. https://www.brainyquote.com/quotes/confucius_393491
68 Stoicism. https://dailystoic.com/
   what-is-stoicism-a-definition-3-stoic-exercises-to-get-you-started/
69 Followers of Stoicism. https://www.entrepreneur.com/article/252625
70 Seneca's birth and death. https://plato.stanford.edu/entries/seneca/
71 The lessons of Seneca. https://medium.com/stoicism-philosophy-as-a-way-of-life/
   lessons-from-seneca-d9e2bb02fdb4
72 Seneca Quote. https://www.business2community.com/workplace-culture/9-life-
   lessons-from-seneca-on-how-to-manage-your-time-effectively-02266411
73 Marcus Aurelius. https://www.history.com/topics/ancient-history/marcus-aurelius
74 Adversity of Marcus Aurelius. https://www.biography.com/political-figure/
   marcus-aurelius
75 IBID.
76 Quotes of Marcus Aurelius. https://erickimphotography.com/blog/marcus-aurelius/
77 Epictetus. https://iep.utm.edu/epictetu/
78 Financial Aid Assistance. Provided by The Citadel Foundation Spring 2021 Fact
   Sheet distribution to all TCF Class Chairmen.
79 Tuition and minority population. IBID.
80 *Esprit de Corps* verse by Author W. Thomas McQueeney, February 18, 2021.
81 Ecclessiates 12:1. KJV. *"Remember now thy Creator in the days of thy youth, while the
   evil days come not, nor the years draw nigh, when thou shalt say, I have no pleasure in
   them"*

*Progress for tomorrow: Capers Hall, demolished in the summer of 2021, is to be replaced by 2023-24.*
*Photo by author.*

## *Other Publications by the Author*
# *W. Thomas McQueeney*

The following books have been published by author W. Thomas McQueeney and are available at most fine bookstores including Barnes & Noble, Apple Books, Ingram Spark, and Amazon. Order by author name or ISBN code. All are also available by *e*Book format for Kindle or other digital technology. The author also stocks all books locally at his place of business—1105 Mazzy Lane, Mount Pleasant, South Carolina 29464. Every publication has a charitable engagement beneficiary as the author has no commercial interest in his avocation. He will be happy to autograph copies for those seeking samples of poor penmanship.

# *The Anthology*
# The Rise of Charleston
### *Conversations with Visionaries, Luminaries & Emissaries of the Holy City*

ISBN 9781625858597.  Paperback. $21.99.  The History Press.
Original Publication 2011 in hardback.
Updated and Reprinted 2017.  312 Pages.

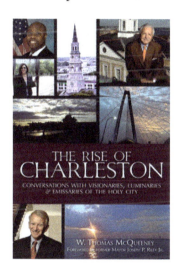

This volume was republished by updating and enhancing the topic from the original hardback version in 2011.  Since its 1670 founding, Charleston has experienced the devastation of wars, economic hardships, and natural disasters. And yet, Charlestonians and their city have prevailed through it all. It is in this current generational surge that the Holy City has experienced meteoric success and taken its place on the world stage. This thematic weave of essays drawn from interviews explores those essential personalities who have lifted Charleston to its new perch as a must-see destination—one that is known as the most welcoming and the most recommended in America. Join engaging local author W. Thomas McQueeney in this updated edition as he relays stories of the 1950s, '60s and '70s through the eyes of those who have witnessed Charleston's evolution to become the charming city it is today.

## Sunsets Over Charleston
### *More Conversations with Visionaries, Luminaries & Emissaries of the Holy City*

ISBN 9781609497859. Hardback. $24.99. The History Press.
Published 2012. 336 Pages.

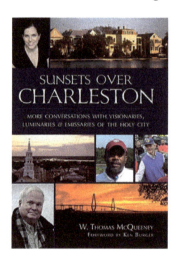

Charleston is among the world's most cherished destinations, and its history is told and retold to the mass of travelers in search of the storied, classical southern ambiance touted in a bygone age. The people of Charleston have witnessed this awakening from within, and author W. Thomas McQueeney presents a glimpse of that shared experience through conversational interviews with some of the city's more notable inhabitants. Explore the area's recent past and present by reading about just some of this city's more interesting personalities who were born in or drawn to a place America has come to love. Each is testament to why the Holy City has become one of the most livable and enjoyable places to be.

# Holy Waters of Charleston
### *The Compelling Influence of Bishop John England & Father Joseph Laurence O'Brien*

ISBN 1626199418.  Hardback.  $19.99. The History Press.
Published 2015. 128 Pages.

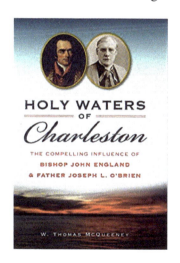

Bishop John England came to Charleston from Ireland in late December 1820. Father Joseph L. O'Brien was ordained a Catholic priest in 1912, and though he served nearly a century after England, his work seamlessly continued much that was started by Charleston's first Catholic bishop. England brought with him a determination to devoutly serve the needs of the Diocese of Charleston, which included South Carolina, North Carolina and Georgia. O'Brien, with the help of Reverend James May, opened Bishop England High School and operated as the school's rector for thirty-two years. England and O'Brien supported and promoted the Catholic Church in Charleston with fervor, bringing together a dedicated community. Author W. Thomas McQueeney details the commitment to service of two of Charleston's most influential Catholic clergy.

## At First Averse and Then Another
### *A Poet Without Pentameters*

ISBN 9780692690970.  Paperback.  $19.99.  Arcadia Publishing.
Published 2016.   226 Pages.

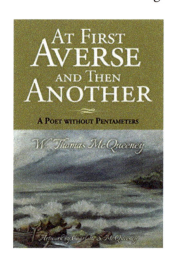

This collection combines the artwork of the late Charleston Renaissance artist Charlotte Simmons McQueeney with the verse renderings of her son, W. Thomas McQueeney.  The artwork illustrates a wide influence of Carolina Lowcountry culture. Mediums include pen and ink, oil, pastel, acrylic and the artist's favorite media, watercolor.  The literary offerings number 121 submissions, mostly filled with satirical musings mindful of the humorists e.e. cummings, Ogden Nash, or Shel Silverstein. Included are other cerebral compositions in the classical genre mindful of writers such as William Butler Yeats or Rod McKuen. This volume is sure to bring a smile and warm the heart.

## Averse Again Now and Then
### *Light Verse From the Pluff Mud Poet*

ISBN 1544281226.  Paperback $19.99.  Arcadia Publishing.
Published 2017.  246 Pages.

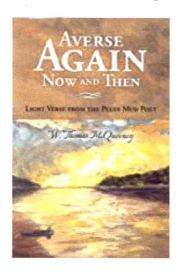

Averse Again Now and Then is a literary compilation of satire, light verse, and humor in classical forms of prose and poetry. A student of literature would find submissions to include the limerick, ode, dramatic monologue, sonnet, haiku, ballad, villanelle, and the poet's favored forms, free verse and metered rhyme. This is the companion volume to *At First Averse and Then Another*. There are artistic submissions interspersed throughout, also the creations of the author. Five chapters are devoted to the curious idiosyncrasies of the fifty states of the United States, portraying each within their historical context. The wit and humor within this volume are intended to entertain the reader—a goal the author intimates as most needed in a digitally saturated, politically divided, and complex world that sometimes loses its way.

## Disaffections of Time
### *A Novel*

ISBN 978-1-9845-1465-3. Paperback. Also available as hardback. XLibris Publishing. $24.99. Published 2017. 416 Pages.

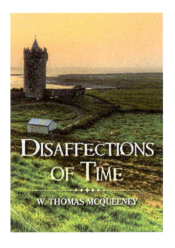

*Disaffections of Time* is a fictional account of a modern wizard-like savant. The charismatic old man utilizes special powers of connecting seemingly unrelated trivia to discern meaningful solutions from his operational base—a coffee shop booth. His reputation enhances a local following. His encounters include a battered housewife, an illegal immigrant with a birth defect, a minority brick mason whose wife is dying, and a hapless bookie pursued by an organized crime syndicate. These encounters lead to dramatic and sometimes humorous interchanges. The major narrative is a compelling tale of romance involving young lovers separated by fate. Their story weaves throughout the novel to be meticulously resolved by the savant. Eventually, the elderly sage must travel forward in time. His exit intrigues. *Disaffections of Time* incorporates modern science, exotic sites, humorous exchanges, and mystical powers within a vividly descriptive literary flow. Romantic settings entice the reader and elevate the alluring sequences with intellectual discourse. The characters, locations, and events were developed from many of the author's wide personal experiences. Though this is his initial novel, the author has written seven previous books. A sequel to *Disaffections of Time* is forthcoming.

## Around in Circles
### *Les Robinson: Life, Basketball, and the NCAA*

ISBN 1641111909.  Paperback.  $39.99.  Palmetto Publishing.
Published 2018.  425 Pages.

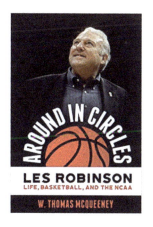

Les Robinson grew up propitiously in St. Albans, West Virginia, where his father organized and hosted the best college basketball players in America to a summer tournament. The Charleston (WV) *Sportsmen's Classic* brought in players like Hot Rod Hundley, Oscar Robertson, Jerry Lucas, Tom Havlicek, Bobby Knight, Elgin Baylor, Bill Russell, and Jerry West. Robinson's career flourished as an Everett Case recruit at N.C. State University. When Case became ill, Coach Press Maravich assumed head coaching duties. Robinson became a coaching protege to Maravich, and a friend to his famous son, Pistol Pete Maravich. After college, Robinson rose through the ranks of college basketball coaches eventually replacing Coach Jim Valvano at his alma mater, N.C. State. There, he coached against the best—Dean Smith, Mike Krzyzewski, and his best friend in the roundball business, Bobby Cremins. Robinson served as head coach and athletic director at three institutions—The Citadel, East Tennessee State, and N.C. State. He also served on the NCAA Selection Committee and the NIT Selection Committee. His recall of stories inside the NCAA experience are both humorous and dynamic. The insightful tales of hundreds of well-known players and coaches included are sure to entertain even the most casual fan.

# Geechee Gonna Gitcha
## *THE FUN-DAMENTAL GUIDE TO CHARLESTON*

ISBN 1641111895.  Paperback $27.99.  Palmetto Press.
Published 2019.  270 Pages.

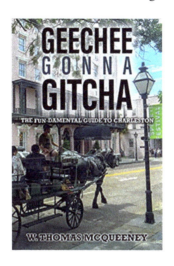

*Geechee Gonna Gitcha* is focused on capturing the essence of the author's native city across time. It defines a city and its people—both
trying to overcome transitional times in a place where the clocks
seemed to be broken. The main character is the setting—Charleston,
South Carolina. Living here through the 1950's and 1960's was a
stark difference to the city seen today. Those decades seemed to be
the time when Charleston woke up and looked out of the window.
We were all Geechees then.  Our Geechee commonality remains in
the "Charlestonese" inflections—and we're losing it faster than the
Wild West lost the bison.  Coming here, one would have no idea of
what once was and still is. The chapters will weave through the realities, the mysteries, and the motives. They are arranged without chro-
nology so that random chapters may be read in any order. The intent
is to give a "cumya" or even a stunned tourist the insight to what this

city represents. The author provides the stark facts related to the history, architecture, culture, celebrities, events, cuisine, language, and horrific natural disasters accentuated with his native smile.

# Growing Up Geechee
## *A Traumatic Comedy*
ISBN 1641113219. Paperback. $36.99. Palmetto Publishing.
Published 2018. 393 Pages.

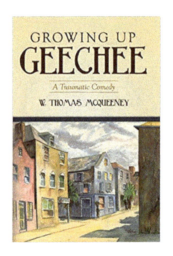

The city that floundered for a century became the incubation chamber for many rocking chair stories of hilarity, insight, warmth, and triumph. The author lived the life-changing moments with the fervor of anticipation within the cozy beginnings of this large Charleston family's journey. This postwar genesis included nine children raised in a loving and resourceful marriage. The four-room "pink house" still exists. It's a story of persistence, discipline, humility, and most of all—humor. One will become enraptured by the Charleston of yesterday when ambiance was an unknown and tourism was where others traveled. Charleston was a map point on hurricane tracking stations—and nothing more. There were a handful of mediocre restaurants, un-air-conditioned hotels, and poorly marketed activities to enjoy. Otherwise, it was too humid, too stark, and too cocooned by the generations that persevered. But the older generations gave it the uniqueness of character that survives to the present. This author's family's journey, though often obstructed by recurrent difficulties, gives insight to the era and life to the process. One should be well entertained by the keen recollections of the times that were both formative and fascinating. Late in the book, the author reaches into the outcomes of the family's fulfillment and Charleston's attainment of worldly nuances. It is an expedition of joy.

## Truth Across the Waters
### *The Admiral Who Changed America*
ISBN 1641117168.  Paperback.  $24.99.  Palmetto Press.
Published 2020.  229 Pages.

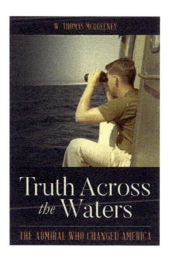

A life built upon truth is often a life of challenge when much is at stake. The life of Admiral William L. Schachte, Jr., navigates the waters of truth in a world where shoals of malfeasance are all too common. From Vietnam Swift Boats—to the Black Sea Incident with the Soviet Russians—to the infamous Tailhook Scandal—one man of character connects all three events. He fought in America's most controversial war, advised our national leaders on international maritime law, and insisted upon proper military decorum throughout his beloved U.S. Navy career. Political historians will validate that Admiral Billy Schachte likely changed the outcome of a U.S. presidential election. He did so by speaking truth in the face of incredible political forces. It was his duty, as he saw it, and not a choice. Our republic's very health depends upon a commitment to the truth as championed throughout the life of a relatively unknown admiral.

## Post Pandemic Perspective
*Positive Projections for the New Normal in the Aftermath of COVID-19*
ISBN 1641118903. Paperback. $12.99. Palmetto Publishing. Published 2020. 136 Pages.

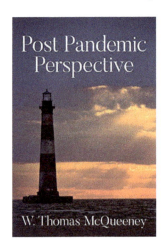

The COVID-19 coronavirus was unanticipated, unwelcome, and unsettling in its far-reaching destruction of life, lifestyles, and the U.S. economy. Its fallout presented Americans with an untimely pause in our busy days, giving us time to contemplate fear of the unseen and unknown. The pandemic would pass, but when? How would it change the United States and, indeed, the world around us? What careers were impacted? What markets were challenged? What will the added debt, both personal and national, portend to the average consumer in the future? When will we gather again in confidence? *Post Pandemic Perspective* attempts to answer these and other important questions that will impact the future of every American. Through meticulous research, W. Thomas McQueeney has scoped out the landscape over the next hill and categorized the major concerns facing us, striving to find the light at the end of the tunnel. He writes with a positive sense of purpose to reassure those who have made it through this epic event that it is still possible to thrive. The post-pandemic reality presents a new beginning that will depend upon the difficult lessons we all will have learned during our days of hardship. Our perspective has been broadened by the experience. We will now demand better ways in all avenues of living—because better ways do exist, in the realms of culture, hygiene, education, religion, government, medicine, finance, and interpersonal relationships. It's true, no joyful birth escapes pain. But while we sadly lament what has happened and the horrid loss of lives to the viruses, we should also be confident in our transition to the exciting world that awaits us ahead.

# Holy Orders Holy Waters
*Re-Exploring the Compelling Influence of Bishop John England*
*And Monsignor Joseph L. O'Brien*
ISBN9781641118880. Hardback. Also available in paperback.
Palmetto Publishing $12.99. Published in 2020. 140 pages.

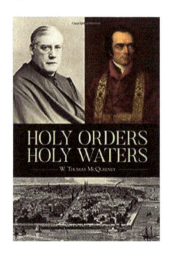

This is an updated version of Holy Waters of Charleston with added chapters in observance of the 200th Anniversary of the Diocese of Charleston. The author traveled to Ireland to complete the research and added the new information discovered.

When the Declaration of Independence was crafted, it revolutionized geo-political thought across the world. Yet it took many years to resolve centuries-old conflicts of race, creed, and class. On the last day of December 1820, the first Catholic Bishop south of Baltimore stepped from a ship to his new home in Charleston, South Carolina. He had arrived from Cork, Ireland. He had scant resources and very few followers of the Catholic Faith to administer. Much changed over the following decades as Bishop John England became the most admired Catholic prelate in the fledgling years of America. When he died in 1842, bells rang out across the city in his honor. Yet no Catholic Church had bells. Nearly a century later, Bishop John England's biographer, himself a priest, emerged in the Holy City as a beacon for education, ethics, and youth development. Monsignor Joseph Lawrence "Doc" O'Brien began the first co-educational high school in Charleston emphasizing the pillars of profound spirituality, physical fitness, and scholastic enterprise. The Pennsylvania native came to a southern city still in decline since the Civil War. He dedicated his life to rebuild the three virtues of Faith, Hope, and Love across a receptive audience. These two priests changed the interaction of divergent faiths in the South—and changed thousands of lives, as well. They are re-discovered in research and recorded warmly for what they achieved.

## Voyages, Passages & Pilgrimages
### *Ruminations from Roaming Other Nations*
ISBN 9781649903204. Paperback. 8"x10". $33.99.
Palmetto Publishing.
Published 2020. 282 pages.

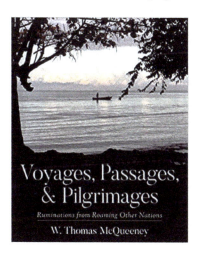

The dawn of global interaction has found its warm sunshine in the past century of international travel. Too often we may pass through without fully appreciating what is there that is different than what we knew from home. In his humorous and insightful exploration, author W. Thomas McQueeney takes you to the cultural diversity, historical characters, and exciting experiences you'll treasure always. Not meant to be a travel guide, but rather a "life's experience guide" to places to be enjoyed and even to be enamored. The author's fourteenth book covers a genre set within his passion for travel. There are personal adventures detailed, international events attended, and the fortunate "happenstance" of genuine friends met along the way. The author's keen sense of humor adds to the travelogue, while it piques the overall interest of the excursion. Unlike the glossy guides, you will be forewarned of places of potential danger, the concern of pickpockets, and the belligerence of many crowded tourist traps. Importantly, this production is also meant for those who may not travel at all. It's a way to bring the reader to the places through the experiences of the author. The presentation is as entertaining as it is informative. The volume contains many amazing photographs and is intended as a coffee-table conversation piece. It is produced in quality design at eight inches by ten inches.